HIGH-IMPACT ENGAGEMENT

A TWO-PHASE APPROACH FOR INDIVIDUAL AND TEAM DEVELOPMENT

TONY LINGHAM, PhD,
AND
BONNIE RICHLEY, PhD

HIGH-IMPACT ENGAGEMENT
A TWO-PHASE APPROACH FOR INDIVIDUAL AND TEAM DEVELOPMENT

iUniverse books may be ordered through booksellers or by contacting:

iUniverse
1663 Liberty Drive
Bloomington, IN 47403
www.iuniverse.com
1-800-Authors (1-800-288-4677)

ISBN: 978-1-5320-4873-9 (sc)
ISBN: 978-1-5320-4874-6 (e)

Library of Congress Control Number: 2018905743

Print information available on the last page.

iUniverse rev. date: 08/30/2018

This book is dedicated to the following:

Chelsea, who joined our family when we were in Barcelona, Spain, as faculty members of ESADE Business School. Her fabulous gentle but firm personality added to the quality of our lives. We found out when she was an adorable six-month-old Pomeranian that she was diagnosed with PDA and had to undergo open-heart surgery immediately or she would die within a year. Despite all her medical issues, Chelsea journeyed with us for ten years—enjoying her life, reading most of our drafts and revisions of articles by sitting on piles of printouts, and eating all the cheese she could. We will always love you and cannot wait to join you on the rainbow bridge.

Rosie, her American-born sister, who is a Pomeranian–toy fox terrier mix. Two years younger than Chelsea, she is still with us at ten years old. She behaves like a perpetual two-year-old and has trained us well to give her everything she wants, including ensuring that she does not have the same food on two consecutive days. She lives on doggie treats and is a very healthy and happy "puppy."

Our cherished family around the world, all of whom have seen us evolve and develop to where we are today, instilling the values we have and the love to help others as a significant part of our purpose in life.

Our dearest close friends, Mary and Jan, who were part of our cohort in our doctoral program. They were among the most beautiful human beings we have ever met, but cancer took them away from us way too soon.

Colleagues, mentors, and students from both Case Western Reserve University and ESADE Business School whose work influenced our growth as engaged scholars, as well as colleagues and others we have collaborated with around the world.

Finally, we dedicate this book to all organizational leaders, team leaders, and educators across the globe who would find this book useful to help develop high-impact engagement wherever they have influence. After all, we are all here to earn our space in life by supporting, caring for, influencing, and challenging employees, students, and others who are a part of our life sphere.

CONTENTS

PREFACE

This book is a culmination of more than two decades of learning, scholarship, and practice—a spiral we call *high-impact learning*. The spiral can be illustrated as follows:

Learning → Teaching → Research and Refinement →
Innovation → Consulting and Refinement → Training

It returns to learning, and the spiral repeats (but is now at a different stage).

In the learning phase, information is gathered from multiple sources in pursuit of understanding in an area or field. In our case, we were deeply immersed in the field of organizational behavior as doctoral students at Case Western Reserve University. This field is structured around four main pillars: experiential learning, competency development, research methods and design, and consulting practice.

During our learning phase, we were exposed to the many theories in the field on individual, team, organizational, and societal levels. The following were the main theories and concepts that influenced our work:

- *experiential learning theory and team theory*, from learning styles, adaptive styles, and conversational learning to our own theories of underlying motivational needs and team interaction

- *competency development*, from managerial competencies to emotional intelligence competencies, and from learning how to develop competency models to eventually collaborating with organizations to develop their own competency and 360-feedback models
- *coaching*, beginning with coaching students, becoming certified senior executive coaches, and eventually functioning as master coaches and trainers for organizations
- *qualitative and quantitative approaches to design and analysis*, from being students to eventually teaching at the doctoral and professional doctoral levels
- *consulting practice*, from learning and practicing appreciative inquiry, learning skills of the organization development practitioner, and being apprentices working with faculty to eventually conducting our own major consulting projects and publishing our work

Throughout this learning phase, we were immersed in the experiential learning cycle specifically by gaining knowledge and developing competencies, from unconscious incompetence to unconscious competence.

As we gained knowledge and skills, we began to teach our own courses at the undergraduate to graduate levels (though mainly at the graduate level). Even as doctoral students, we were nominated for teaching excellence at the undergraduate and graduate levels. Since then, as members of the faculty at national and international universities, we have been nominated for teaching excellence at the graduate and doctoral levels. As faculty, we have also taught in business/management schools, in medical and nursing schools, and in programs that are multidisciplinary in nature.

In the research and refinement phase, we were taught multiple designs and analytical approaches in both qualitative and quantitative methodologies. During this phase, we amassed expertise in qualitative research, from grounded theory to phenomenology, and in quantitative research, from multivariate to measurement theory and methods. We have also been trained in, conducted, and published research that uses sequential mixed methods. As faculty, we have taught qualitative, quantitative, and mixed methods at the doctoral level (both management and multidisciplinary programs, and both nationally and internationally).

In this book, we have used mixed methods but primarily measurement theory and methods, and we have paid close attention to the standards of rigor and ethics in our research. In alignment with measurement theory and methods, we made sure we refined our measures by focusing on establishing clean dimensions and testing for reliability and validity. Further refinement was established as we used our scales in other contexts in the US and other countries across the globe to establish the robustness of our measures.

As we were conducting our research, we were also paying attention to unexpected findings and anything else the results might be indicating to us. Based on these findings as feedback, we explored better framing and presentation to meet organizational and educational needs at the individual and team levels, and we developed a method to use this in training and development programs. Finally, we further developed the design summit as an approach for organizational-level change and development.

As we started using this approach as an offering for creating, leading, and sustaining high-impact teams in organizations, feedback from participants helped us further develop our method and provide information from the data to facilitate individual- and team-level coaching as part of the training process. Using this approach, we were able to provide evidence-based coaching. Discussions with participants during training and coaching sessions revealed that our approach is a powerful method for developing and improving engagement at the individual, interpersonal, and team levels, which in turn influenced their organizations.

Through the years, we have been able to present our method as a two-phase approach to creating and sustaining high-impact engagement, incorporating effective coaching for individuals, team leaders, and teams. We have used this approach for numerous organizations worldwide and across diverse industries including for-profit, nonprofit, multinational companies, and educational institutions. This book is the result of our own spiral of high-impact learning and can have a meaningful and powerful impact on organizations and educational institutions. We hope this book will show the high quality, credibility, strength, and evidence of our two-phase approach.

ACKNOWLEDGMENTS

This book is a result of our high-impact learning process through the years as academics, scholars, consultants, and practitioners. Throughout this process, we have met many wonderful people who offered ideas to refine our thinking and approach. We had our own experience of high-impact engagement, with the added benefit of collaborating with family, friends, colleagues, students, organizational leaders, and members who all also gave our lives meaning.

We also would like to acknowledge our dear friends who believe in what we do and encouraged the writing of this book. Engaging with people is such a wonderful experience when there is bidirectional care, support, and belief throughout, resulting in outcomes that surpass our own capacities and capabilities. This book is richer and better from our high-impact engagement with such wonderful people.

We hope that this book will be of help as a part of creating wonderful and positive high-impact teams, which in turn will result in high-impact engagement. We do believe that such engagement will help us all develop into better human beings cognitively, physically, emotionally, and spiritually. May we all live blessed, wonderful, joyous, and meaningful lives despite the challenges life throws at us.

CHAPTER 1

Introduction

1.1 Our Evolving Organizational and Educational Environments

The experience of change has never been so fast paced and chaotic as it has been in the last few decades. Organizations increasingly have to innovate and evolve to thrive in such an unpredictable and competitive landscape. To meet this challenge, most organizations have moved to a team-oriented structure across all levels, creating the need for people to be able to work effectively with others in multiple settings.

The need to work effectively has been the driving force for our work for more than eighteen years with individuals and teams across the globe. This book provides a scientifically supported methodology for organizations and educational institutions to effectively help employees and students develop these skills so as to effectively engage with others or in a team.

Educational institutions have aligned with this shift and incorporated more assignments and projects into their curriculum that require teamwork. Just as organizations are experiencing an influx of multiple cultures into their workforce, educational institutions across the globe are also experiencing more foreign or international students studying and working alongside domestic students. With the integration of technology and the fusion of the virtual and physical worlds of work, the need to evolve faster to survive and thrive is unprecedented.

1.2 Diversity Is Taking Multiple Forms

Diversity has evolved beyond just race and gender. In today's world, diversity takes multiple forms. With the collapsing of national and geographical boundaries, diversity is now also experienced as understanding people from different nations and with different cultural norms and expectations. This need has resulted in cultural awareness programs in organizations and educational institutions. These programs range from language classes to understanding diverse perspectives when working with others.

Technological advancements, social media, and the internet have created a fusion of physical and virtual environments. Working well with the five generations that exist in today's workforce has proven to be not as easy as we expected. We have generational differences not only in age but also in terms of how savvy people are in combining physical and virtual work and home lives.

Today, we interact with others in very different ways. We are becoming far more complex as humans than ever before. In fact, we no longer have a diverse workforce. We now have a complex workforce. We will therefore need to develop the sensitivity and skill to work with such a complex workforce, be it as colleagues or in a team.

> We no longer have a diverse workforce. We now have a complex workforce.

1.3 Teams Have Become a Fundamental Way of Work

The need to evolve and adapt to this unpredictable work context has led to the increase of teams in organizations. The increasing need to innovate and design new approaches to work has resulted in more cross-functional, inter-professional, multicultural, multinational teams and think tanks in organizations. Teams are everywhere. In fact, most organizations are designed with a team approach in mind. A 2016 study done by Deloitte[1] indicated that globally, organizations are shifting toward a team-oriented design and considering this a very important approach in today's global work environment. As a result, one will find teams across all levels in an organization, from boards and top management teams to ad hoc and work teams creating a network of teams. Inherent in this team structure is a unique design where a team leader on one team may be a team member on a team at a higher level, or a team member on one team could be a team leader on a team at a lower level.

To add to this, employees may find themselves on multiple teams. People do not work alone. Educational institutions have included more teamwork in their curriculum, with some courses designed exclusively for teamwork. Being able to lead and work in teams is becoming a norm more than a desired skill.

Organizations are certainly pushing for individuals and teams to have skills to innovate and execute effectively. They need a strong and engaged workforce to ensure their success. This has created the need to have people develop the skills to both work on a team and to lead a team. A recent study[2] showed that out of 10,640 projects from 200 companies in thirty countries, only 2.5 percent of companies fulfilled 100 percent of their projects. So although teams are ubiquitous, most are not as effective as desired. Questions that

> The majority of work done in organizations is done in teams.

---

[1] T. McDowell, D. Agarwal, D. Miller, T. Okamoto, and T. Page, "Organizational Design: The Rise of Teams," Deloitte Insights, February 29, 2016, https://www2.deloitte.com/insights/us/en/focus/human-capital-trends/2016/organizational-models-network-of-teams.html.

[2] B. Hardy-Vallee, "The Cost of Bad Project Management," *Gallup Business Journal*, February 7, 2012, http://news.gallup.com/businessjournal/152429/Cost-Bad-Project-Management.aspx.

have emerged include "How do we help a team become a team?" and "What happens when we are a team in crisis?"

The two-phase approach presented in this book is designed to help individuals and teams shift from a focus on completing tasks to contributing effectively to a larger system, such as department, division, functional group, top management team, and the organization as a whole. To help individuals develop this capacity, we focus on a solid awareness and understanding of underlying motivations and capacities when working together and creating high-quality engagement at the interpersonal and team levels.

We believe that teams are not just people coming together to complete a task. They are living entities in an organization and should be developed in their own specific work contexts. As one of us stated: Teams are engines that drive businesses; they are the force bringing innovations to life; and they are the central organizing concept for all work relationships.

> Teams are engines that drive businesses; they are the force bringing innovations to life; and they are the central organizing concept for all work relationships.

1.4 No One Works Alone

The days of the solitary genius are past. We encounter many people who would like to work alone, but that is not going to happen. Projects or tasks are assigned to teams, committees, pairs, or some other configuration, but they are not done exclusively by one individual. We must have an ability to work with very different people not just occasionally but almost always. We may be assigned to work with others from across the globe through virtual platforms or communication modes (such as Zoom, GoToMeeting, AdobeConnect, WebEx, and FaceTime) while also working with people within our organization. Flextime is another innovation in the work environment that creates the need to work with others through multiple modes instead of just face-to-face.

All these forms of technology are presenting a wide variety of ways for individuals to work with others. In today's world, people no longer work alone. This has certainly presented a need to help individuals develop the ability and sensitivity to work with very different people, sometimes even within a workday. Individuals are always working with others in some shape or form.

> People do not work alone anymore. We are constantly working with others in some shape or form.

1.5 Self- and Other- Awareness

Developing self-awareness and other-awareness is a critical first step in creating higher levels of engagement when working with others or on multiple teams. Although there are a plethora of training programs to develop individuals in organizations and educational institutions, extending this to help individuals develop an equal capacity of other-awareness is vital. The value of training programs that help individuals develop self- and other-awareness cannot be understated, and these should be a prerequisite for training and development at the team level to help employees work and engage effectively in teams.

Developing the skills to lead and work in teams is certainly a critical need for organizations and educational institutions, as the majority of work done in organizations is done in teams. Yet most training programs are focused on the individual level, with very few on how individual awareness is linked to

> Most training programs are focused on the individual level, with very few on how individual awareness is linked to awareness at the interpersonal and team levels.

5

awareness at the interpersonal and team levels. According to a report[3] from the American Society of Training and Development, an estimate of about $156 million was spent in 2011 on employee learning and development. With organizations moving toward team-oriented designs, being able to work with others interpersonally and at the team level requires knowledge of how to positively influence working relationships to generate high-impact engagement for organizational success.

---

[3] L. Miller, "ASTD 2012 State of the Industry Report: Organisations Continue to Invest in Workplace Learning," *American Society for Training and Development* (2012): 42–48.

Summary

Our current work environment is evolving at a rapid rate due to advancements in technology, an increasingly complex workforce, and increasingly diverse ways to interact with others. We can summarize these shifts as follows:

1. Work involves working with others and working in teams.
2. Most training efforts are focused on the individual and not enough on the team.
3. Globally, organizations are shifting to become team-oriented in their structural design.
4. Most work done in organizations is done in teams. However, a recent study of 10,640 projects from 200 companies globally showed that only 2.5 percent of organizations completed 100 percent of their tasks.
5. We are all engaged on multiple teams.
6. High-impact engagement involves innovation and execution, which are critical to organizational success.

Our Approach to High-Impact Engagement

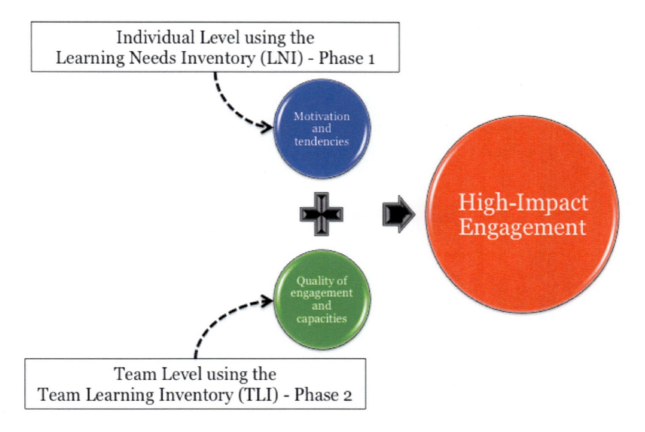

CHAPTER 2

High-Impact Engagement: What This Means to Us as Individuals Working with Others or with a Team

2.1 The Centrality of Teamwork

In today's world, as most work is done in teams, the ability to lead teams or work effectively in teams is critical. We must develop high-impact engagement in such a way that members can contribute to and influence organizational performance. It certainly matters if we are able to influence teams, organizations, or larger systems in ways that increase energy and drive to ensure evolution and success. Instead, all too often, we hear of frustrations when working with others or experiencing how others do not listen enough to understand individuals or allow them to contribute positively. Whether in organizations or educational institutions, teamwork is becoming central, and high-impact engagement is not just necessary but critical to evolving and thriving in this environment

2.2 What This Means to Us as Individuals

It is a common and accepted fact that change is constant. In organizations, the ability of individuals to adapt, innovate, and execute effectively is key to being successful. These abilities are also critical when working with others, especially since organizations are increasingly becoming team oriented in structure and function. Working successfully with others in a team environment requires knowledge of one's adaptability

> Individuals have to be more adaptive and have the ability to innovate and execute effectively.

to changes both in the work itself and in the need of the organization to thrive in our current volatile environment. It is equally important to develop innovation and execution skills to be an effective leader, manager, and employee.

2.3 Learning to Engage with Others at Work and in Educational Institutions

As organizations and educational institutions evolve to adapt to the constantly changing external environment, adaptability is critical for employee and student development. A good employee is not one who is able to contribute as long as nothing much changes. In fact, a good employee is one who can easily and readily adapt to the constant change of demands of the job, tasks, and relationships in the work environment.

In the educational context, a student who is ready to enter and succeed in the work environment upon graduation is one who can work effectively with others as part of a team or multiple teams while working on a multitude of projects. Developing skills that promote or

> Individuals have to be trained to adapt to constant changes when engaging with others.

facilitate effective engagement would make organizations stronger and more resilient. Let us begin by discussing learning and its link to adaptability.

2.4 Knowing How We Learn

We are engaging in learning and development whenever we do something for the first time. Some people may want to get things done quickly, while others will want to ensure that everything is in place before taking action. According to David Kolb's experiential learning theory,[4]

> Individuals learn in different ways when they engage with something new for the first time.

there are four major learning styles that individuals prefer to use based on how they take in and use information. These preferred learning styles are diverging, assimilating, converging, and accommodating. They can be described as follows:

1. *Diverging*—People with the diverging learning style tend to gather information from within the context and reflect on the information gathered before proceeding along the learning cycle.

2. *Assimilating*—Those with the assimilating learning style tend to gather information by conceptualizing and reflecting on the information gathered before moving through the cycle of learning.

3. *Converging*—Individuals with the converging learning style gather information by conceptualizing and using this information by acting on it.

4. *Accommodating*—Those with the accommodating learning style will first gather information from within the context and then act on it as the initial approach before entering the learning cycle.

---

[4] D. A. Kolb, *Experiential Learning: Experience as a Source of Learning and Development* (Englewood Cliffs, NJ: Prentice-Hall Inc., 1984).

The diagram below shows how the four styles are determined based on the combination of "grasping" or gathering information and "transforming" or using information.[5]

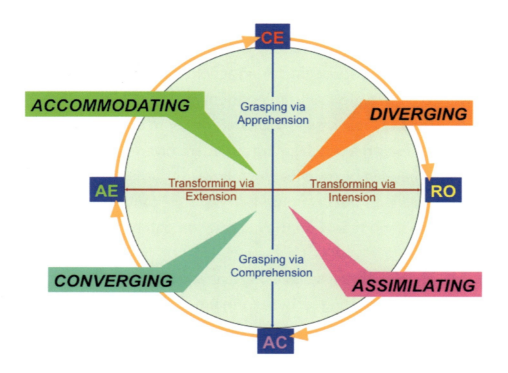

Individuals could also advise others on how to work through struggles at work by suggesting what has worked for them, not realizing that the other person may have a completely different learning style (or a learning style that is diametrically opposed). One might see this in both organizational and educational settings when supervisors or faculty say things like "You just have to learn by watching others" or "Just plunge into the work/project and learn from the mistakes you make." The former advice is based on a diverging learning style while the latter

_____
[5] For a succinct description of experiential learning theory and proposed future directions, see T. Lingham, "Experiential Learning Theory," in *International Encyclopedia of Organization Studies*, eds. S. Clegg and J. R. Bailey (Thousand Oaks, CA: Sage Publications, 2008), 487–92.

is based on an assimilating learning style. Advice or assistance that aligns with an individual's learning style is more effective than approaches that are different. In essence, knowing one's own preferred learning style is one side of the coin and knowing others' preferred learning styles is the other. Getting people to understand these two sides would improve learning and development.

2.5 Knowing How to Listen

We are familiar with the following exchanges when working with others:

- "Can we stop this discussion? It is wasting time. Could we go on to what we should be doing?"
- "Why are you being such a pain by always asking for clarification?"
- "Are you sure this is aligning with what is expected of us?"

All too often, we respond to these questions positively or negatively depending on their relevance to the task; our own interests and concerns; or what is important to us. When we get frustrated with individuals on teams who constantly do not resonate with us, we classify our relationship as a personality clash or tag them as being difficult to work with. This is absolutely not a way to achieve high-impact engagement! No one wants to come to work to hurt or alienate others. We all want to feel valued and appreciated for what we do or contribute.

For the past eighteen years—as trainers, consultants, and educators—we have been getting executives, leaders, managers, and students to understand different learning styles so they can work more effectively with others. Over time, we began to realize that there is something much deeper underlying learning styles that is central and even critical to helping people work together effectively. When engaging with others, it is more important to listen

> We need to listen to how people frame questions or statements when engaging with them.

to how they frame statements than just paying attention to what they say. This deeper level can also be observed by how people behave when working with others in the work environment. It is from this that we began to develop our learning needs theory of motivation[6] that links learning styles, work motivation, and creativity/innovation. This knowledge will allow you to develop quality engagement and positively impact individuals, teams, and the larger system.

2.6 What It Means to Us When Working in a Team

Creating high-impact engagement at the team level is exponentially more complex than engaging with individuals, as we have to take into account and embrace the complexity and diversity of team members. The quality of engagement at the team level involves a team's ability to function and perform effectively. We have heard of training programs that focus on developing high-functioning teams or high-performing teams and seldom those that focus on both aspects of teamwork.

This book is designed to help teams become high-impact teams (HITs)—teams that are high-functioning and high-performing while also having the capacity to influence the department, division, and organization. Developing HITs involves diving into the actual and desired experiences of teamwork so as to surface the quality of individuals' engagement and team-level capacity to both innovate and execute.

> High-impact teams (HITs) are both high-functioning and high-performing while also being able to influence the larger system.

[6] T. Lingham, "A Learning Needs Theory of Motivation," *Organization and Management* 4, no. 8 (2010): 103–15.

2.7 Quality of Team Engagement

We have heard team members complaining about how difficult working with a team is or how wonderful it was working with a team. More interestingly, a member of two or more teams might express very different experiences across these teams. Understanding the experience of teamwork would certainly offer the possibility of helping teams to thrive.

Researchers[7] of teams and teamwork have recently highlighted the importance of understanding the experience of team interaction in the work environment. In this book, we will elaborate on how the experience of teamwork can be captured based on how team members interact with each other. The profile based on this measure provides teams with the quality of their engagement based on actual and desired interactions at any one point in time.

> A team's experience of interaction generates the quality of team engagement.

2.8 A Team's Capacity to Both Innovate and Execute

Since the 1950s, the use of teams has evolved from sporadic to ubiquitous across the globe. There are two major reasons for this trend: teams (when effective) are far superior to individuals in helping organizations thrive in a volatile environment, and teams have tremendous capacity to generate outcomes that are innovative while also having the ability to execute decisions and

---

[7] Some examples are as follows: A. P. Hare, "Roles, Relationships, and Groups in Organizations: Some Conclusions and Recommendations," *Small Group Research* 34, no. 2 (2003): 123–54; G. W. Wittenbaum, A. B. Hollingshead, P. B. Paulus, R. Y. Hirokawa, D. G. Ancona, R. S. Peterson, K. A. Jehn, and K. Yoon, "The Functional Perspective as a Lens for Understanding Groups," *Small Group Research* 35, no. 1 (2004): 17–43; J. Bradley, B. J. White, and B. E. Mennecke, "Teams and Tasks: A Temporal Framework for the Effects of Interpersonal Interventions on Team Performance," *Small Group Research* 34, no. 3 (2003): 353–87; A. Seers and S. Woodruff, "Temporal Pacing in Task Forces: Group Development or Deadline Pressure?" *Journal of Management* 23, no. 2 (1997): 169–87.

tasks. Making an impact at the organizational level requires the ability to innovate and execute in ways that positively influence the system in which the team is embedded (department, division, or organization), thereby increasing the organization's capacity to succeed and thrive.

> Teams have tremendous capacity to innovate and execute to positively influence an organization's ability to thrive.

2.9 High-Impact Engagement

What is high-impact engagement? It is a melding of both the individual and team levels. In this book, we focus on two phases in achieving high-impact engagement:

1. *Understanding individual motivations and tendencies when with others*—In the next chapter, we will dive deeper into four fundamental motivational needs that unconsciously drive each of us when working with others in our work environment. In phase 1 of achieving high-impact engagement, we also administer our Learning Needs Inventory to profile individuals' adaptability and also their innovation and execution tendencies.

2. *Capturing a team's engagement profiles and capacities to innovate and execute*—In phase 2 of the book, we dive deeper into capturing the actual and desired engagement profiles and capacities of a team in a work context. We administer the Team Learning Inventory to focus on the team level and help teams understand how to best develop higher-level engagement and improve their capacity to innovate and execute.

The purpose of this book is to help organizations and educational institutions focus on a reliable, valid, and robust method to help employees and students develop the skills needed to effectively engage with others, leading to improved performance. The book is based on over eighteen years of work in multiple organizational and educational contexts and in different countries across the globe.

Summary

As teams have become the primary mode of work, the need to lead and work effectively in teams is critical to organizational success. Developing high-impact teams (HITs) requires training and development at the individual and team levels.

At the Individual Level:

1. We have to be more adaptive and have the ability to innovate and execute effectively.
2. We have to be trained to adapt to constant changes when engaging with others.
3. We have to understand that we all learn in different ways when we engage with something for the first time.
4. We have to listen to how people frame questions or statements when engaging with them.

At the Team Level:

1. We need to be able to lead and work effectively in teams to develop HITs. Such teams are both high-functioning and high-performing; they also have the capacity to positively influence the larger system.
2. We need to be able to create positive team interaction, as this is directly linked to the quality of team engagement.
3. As teams have tremendous capacity to innovate and execute to positively influence an organization's ability to thrive, we need to be able to develop their capacity to innovate and execute.

A Reflective Exercise

We all work in different contexts. Whether you are a consultant, working inside an organization, or volunteering inside an organization, take a moment to think about the challenges you face when creating positive organizational change that sticks and is sustainable.

What are you doing that makes this work?

_____

_____

_____

What did you do to create a high-quality engaged team or workforce?

_____

_____

_____

How could you have worked together to develop as a team?

_____

_____

_____

What are your personal strengths?

_____

_____

_____

What are your weaknesses?

_____

_____

_____

How could you help your weaknesses go away?

_____

_____

_____

Are you aware of others' strengths and weaknesses?

_____

_____

_____

How could you work to develop as an individual?

_____

_____

_____

Phase 1

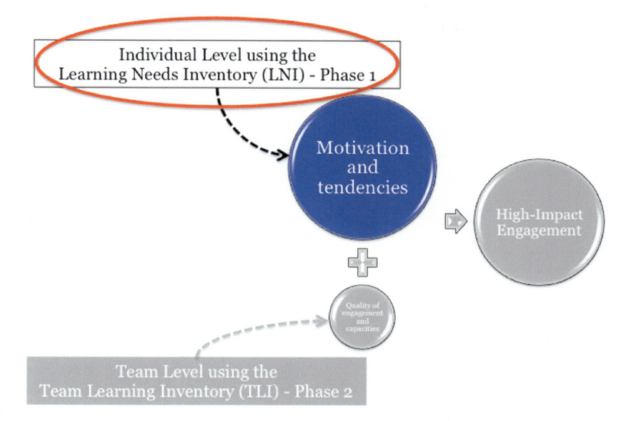

Individual Level using the
Learning Needs Inventory (LNI) - Phase 1

Motivation
and
tendencies

High-Impact
Engagement

Quality of
engagement
and
capacities

Team Level using the
Team Learning Inventory (TLI) - Phase 2

Individual Level

1. Understanding our underlying motivations and tendencies
2. Engaging effectively at the interpersonal level

CHAPTER 3

Transitioning Learning Styles to Underlying Learning Needs of Motivation

3.1 Critique of Learning Styles

What we realized over the initial few years of working with learning styles was that the knowledge perspective (grasping and transforming knowledge) was only the tip of the iceberg. Furthermore, a major UK study[8] in 2004 that focused on reviewing and evaluating the different learning theories claimed that Kolb's four learning styles could not be validated empirically when transformed to a scale so as to be able to test for the four factors in his framework. Only two or three styles (factors) emerged, not four. Having worked with the four styles and finding that they were meaningful to students and executives, we spent seven months trying to uncover a phenomenon underlying these four styles.

---

[8] F. Coffield, D. Moseley, E. Hall, and K. Ecclestone, *Learning Styles and Pedagogy in Post-16 Learning: A Systematic and Critical Review* (London: Learning and Skills Research Center, 2004), available online at http://www.LSRC.ac.uk.

After years of testing and refining, we did indeed find four underlying needs for each style, which inspired us to establish a valid, reliable, and robust scale to distinguish each style based on our expertise, research methods, and measurement theory. Details of the process and analyses we used in developing the Learning Needs Inventory (LNI) are presented in appendix A at the end of this book.

We found that underlying each learning style is a motivational need that has far more impact on efforts to learn how to work effectively with others. We identified four basic needs: information, clarity, parameters, and action. We also confirmed that with the four underlying needs, we were able to further identify how an individual's

> Underlying each learning style is a *motivational need* that has far more impact in learning how to work effectively with others

specific behaviors or framing demonstrate various levels of these needs. We dive deeper into the four underlying needs below.

3.2 The Four Underlying Motivational Learning Needs

3.2.1. Underlying Need for Information (The Explorer)

Individuals with this underlying need tend to push to obtain or explore information from multiple sources—getting ideas from others, and getting information so as to exceed expectations and obtain diverse perspectives. They push for idea generation. Each of the four aspects within the need for information can be identified by how individuals frame questions or act when they are working with others:

1. *Need to gather information from multiple sources*—A person with a high need for this aspect would push to obtain information from as many sources as feasible so as to feel that enough information is uncovered to work with. In a team setting, such an individual

would say things like, "Could we use the internet to see what information is out there?" or "I think we need to expand our search to include other sources" or "Could we observe others to see what they are doing and what we may be missing?"

2. *Need to gather ideas from others*—A person with a high need for this aspect would push to ensure that as many ideas as possible are obtained from every member on the team or to take the time to reflect on these ideas with the intent to surface more ideas. In a team setting, such an individual would say things like "What ideas do you have?" or "Does anyone have other ideas?" or "What other thoughts do people have?" or "We need to put more ideas on the table to work with."

3. *Need to gather information to exceed expectations*—A person with a high need for this aspect would push to obtain as much information as possible to understand expectations with the intent to exceed expectations for projects or tasks given by supervisors, managers, or faculty. This individual would think through the expectations given so as to find ways to exceed them. In a team setting, such an individual would say things like "What are you [supervisor or instructor] expecting from us?" or "We have been given these expectations, but what do you all think about how to exceed them?" or "What can we do to surprise people [our supervisor or instructor] about what we can do?"

4. *Need to gather multiple perspectives*—A person with a high need for this aspect would push to gather information by obtaining and/or listening to the perspectives of others to gain an expanded world view or perspective on projects, topics, or assignments. At the individual level, such a person would reflect and look at matters, issues, or assignments from multiple points of view or seek to obtain perspectives from family, friends, or colleagues. In a team setting, such an individual would say things like "What is your opinion on _____?" or "Anyone have reactions to _____?" or "Anyone have other points of view?" or "What do you understand by _____?"

3.2.2. Underlying Need for Clarity (The Clarifier)

Individuals with this underlying need tend to push to ensure clarity and purpose by working systematically so as to be thorough, developing concrete plans, establishing clear criteria and/or expectations, and ensuring that no one is confused. They push for clarity and purpose, which could lead to buy-in from others. Each of the four aspects within the need for clarity can be identified by how individuals frame questions or act when they are working with others:

1. *Need to ensure clarity by working systematically and thoroughly*—Individuals with a high need for this aspect would push to ensure that they or others work systematically to make sure things are thoroughly worked through. At the individual level, such a person would take the time to work through projects and assignments deliberately and carefully to ensure clarity and thoroughness. In a team setting, such an individual would say things like "Shouldn't we go through this step by step to make sure we cover everything required?" or "I feel like we are pushing this fast and not thinking it through systematically" or "I don't think we have thought or worked through _____ thoroughly."

2. *Need to ensure clarity when developing concrete plans*—A person with a high need for this aspect would push for clear and concrete plans so as to ensure that everyone understands what needs to be done and how it should be done. At the individual level, such a person would take the time to create or establish a clear plan. In a team setting, such an individual would say things like "I am still unclear as to what our plan is" or "Can we go through the plan again so everyone knows what needs to be done and how we plan do it?"

3. *Need to ensure clarity when developing criteria or expectations*—A person with a high need for this aspect would push for clear criteria and/or expectations so as to ensure that everyone understands what has to be considered or what is expected. At the individual level, such a person would take the time to ask questions so as to clarify expectations or

what needs to be considered when working on any assignment. In a team setting, such an individual would say things like "I need to understand what is expected of us and why" or "I am not sure I understand why we need to consider these criteria to get _____ done" or "Can we go through the criteria given to us and what is expected of us again?"

4. *Need to ensure no confusion*—A person with a high need for this aspect would push to ensure that no one is confused about the purpose, goals, expectations, plans, and action to complete projects, tasks, or assignments. At the individual level, such a person would take the time to clear up any confusion or misunderstandings regarding any aspects of the assigned project or task. In a team setting, such an individual would say things like "Is anyone confused about what is expected of us?" or "I think we need to make sure everyone is clear about _____" or "Can we go through the _____ once again so everyone is not confused?" or "I am still confused about _____, so can we revisit that?"

3.2.3. Underlying Need for Parameters (The Selector)

Individuals with this underlying need tend to push to adhere to clear goals and expectations; ensure that there are some criteria and expectations to adhere to; and follow clear guidelines. They seek confirmation that ideas, tasks, and choices made conform to or are aligned with given goals and guidelines and help select the best approach. Each of the four aspects within the need for parameters can be identified by how individuals frame questions or act when they are working with others:

1. *Need to adhere to clear goals*—A person with a high need for this aspect would push to ensure that given goals are clear. At the individual level, such a person would take the time to check with clients, supervisors, leaders, or instructors so as to get clear goals to adhere to. In a team setting, such an individual would say things like "Can we check to make sure we know what our goal is?" or "Do we know anything about the goal given

to us?" or "We need to verify if this is what our [client/supervisor/leader/instructor] wants as the goal of this [project/task/assignment]" or "Can we revisit our goals so as to verify that they are aligned with the goals given to us?"

2. *Need to adhere to clear expectations*—A person with a high need for this aspect would push to ensure expectations that are given are clear. At the individual level, such a person would take the time to ensure that the expectations given are clear so as to adhere to them. In a team setting, such an individual would say things like "Can we check to make sure we know if we have been given clear expectations so we can get this done right?" or "We need to clarify the expectations given to us so that we can adhere to them while working on this assignment" or "I don't think we are working to meet the expectations given to us."

3. *Need to obtain some criteria and expectations to adhere to*—A person with a high need for this aspect would push to ensure that at least some criteria or expectations are given by clients, supervisors, leaders, or instructors. At the individual level, such a person would take the time to ask for some criteria and/or expectations before beginning work on the assignment. In a team setting, such an individual would say things like "Can we get some criteria for this?" or "Do we have any criteria or expectations for this?" or "We need to ensure we have at least some criteria and expectations given to us."

4. *Need to obtain clear guidelines*—A person with a high need for this aspect would push to ensure that work done adheres to the guidelines given. At the individual level, such a person would take the time to clarify the guidelines given by clients, supervisors, leaders, or instructors so as to be able to adhere to the given guidelines. In a team setting, such an individual would say things like "Can we take some time to make sure we are following the guidelines given?" or "Can we go back and clarify that our plan aligns with

the guidelines before proceeding?" or "I am still not quite sure how our plan [or action plan] aligns with the guidelines given to us."

3.2.4. Underlying Need for Action (The Completer)

Individuals with this underlying need tend to push to get tasks done fast, maintain momentum when getting tasks done, get the urgent tasks done first, and try for no (or minimal) delays when getting things done. They push for task completion. Each of the four aspects within the need for action can be identified by how individuals frame questions or act when they are working with others:

1. *Need to get tasks done fast*—A person with a high need for this aspect would push to ensure that things are done fast. At the individual level, such a person would focus on getting tasks done fast so as to get them done as quickly as possible. In a team setting, such an individual would say things like "Can we just move ahead and proceed with the next task?" or "I don't think we are getting things done fast enough" or "We need to do the work fast and not waste more time discussing or talking about _____" or "Can we just focus on getting our tasks done now?"

2. *Need to maintain momentum when getting things done*—A person with a high need for this aspect would push to ensure momentum when doing tasks. At the individual level, such a person would focus on getting tasks done constantly or regularly enough to maintain momentum. In a team setting, such an individual would say things like "Can we press on so as not to lose the pace we have set?" or "I don't think we are maintaining a good pace in getting things done" or "We need to create an action plan that ensures we keep tasks ongoing and at a good pace" or "Can we just focus on getting our tasks done? I think we are losing our momentum."

3. *Need to get urgent tasks done first*—A person with a high need for this aspect would push to work on or focus on urgent tasks. At the individual level, such a person would focus on prioritizing work based on urgency instead of importance. In a team setting, such an individual would say things like "Can we focus on the urgent things that need to be done first?" or "I don't think we are looking at what is urgent that needs to be done" or "I think we should work on _____, _____, and _____, as these are more urgent and therefore need to be done first" or "I'd rather work on the urgent tasks so we can get those out of the way first."

4. *Need to ensure no (or minimal) delays when getting things done*—A person with a high need for this aspect would push to ensure that any delays are kept to a minimum or push to eradicate any delays when working on assignments. At the individual level, such a person would focus on the time it takes to get work done or make sure things do not take too long to get done. In a team setting, such an individual would say things like "Can you make sure you get this done immediately, as it is causing delays in completing _____ on time?" or "I think you are taking too long to get this done, and it is affecting our work" or "We need to get our tasks done on time so we can meet the deadline" or "Can we identify the time it would take to complete each task so as not to cause any delays?"

3.3 Attending to Framing When Working with Others

We present these four fundamental learning needs and the way questions may be framed or how people may act when working together as a technique to effectively work with others. Just paying attention to how people ask questions or push to get others to behave would give us truly valuable real-time insight into how to work effectively with others. When we address the needs others have, they feel more included and heard. This in turn promotes engagement and energy in the team.

It is also important to know that although people may have a tendency to prematurely categorize others, every individual has needs that fall under more than one fundamental need. As a result, it is important to pay attention to the questions at any point in time to adjust to the needs of the individuals on the team, as every individual may surface different needs when going through different phases of projects or work. However, people tend to push for similar needs, and hence the ability to have a profile of learning needs would prove significant for increasing awareness of self and others. The LNI profiles an individual's learning needs and innovation and execution capacities. In the next chapter, we will discuss the LNI in greater detail and demonstrate how it can be a very useful tool for achieving effective engagement with others.

Summary

When we engage with others when working on tasks or projects in the work environment, four fundamental needs drive the way we inquire, behave, and react. These are:

1. **Underlying Need for Information**—Individuals with this underlying need tend to push to obtain or explore information from multiple sources to get ideas from others, gain information so as to exceed expectations, and obtain diverse perspectives.

2. **Underlying Need for Clarity**—Individuals with this underlying need tend to push to ensure clarity and purpose by working systematically so as to be thorough, developing concrete plans, establishing clear criteria and/or expectations, and ensuring that no one is confused.

3. **Underlying Need for Parameters**—Individuals with this underlying need tend to push to adhere to clear goals and expectations; ensure that there are some criteria and expectations to adhere to; and adhere to clear guidelines.

4. **Underlying Need for Action**—Individuals with this underlying need tend to push to get tasks done fast, maintain momentum when getting tasks done, get urgent tasks done first, and try for no (or minimal) delays when getting things done.

Just paying attention to how individuals ask questions or push to get others to behave (positively or negatively) gives truly valuable real-time insight into how to work effectively with others.

A Reflective Exercise

Think about how you engage with others in your work or educational environment. When working on projects on a team, how often do you focus on the following? Circle one option for each.

1. Getting information

   Not often   Often   Very often

2. Ensuring clarity

   Not often   Often   Very often

3. Obtaining clear parameters, guidelines, or expectations

   Not often   Often   Very often

4. Getting things done

   Not often   Often   Very often

Based on your response above, how often do you encounter frustrations from team members or others over the following issues?

5. You focus on getting too much information.

   Not often   Often   Very often

If you answered "very often," how did you react to or deal with the frustrations from others?

_____

6. You focus too much on getting clarity.

   Not often   Often   Very often

If you answered "very often," how did you react to or deal with the frustrations from others?

_____

7. You focus too much on adhering to expectations.

   Not often   Often   Very often

If you answered "very often," how did you react to or deal with the frustrations from others?

_____

8. You focus on getting things done.

   Not often   Often   Very often

If you answered "very often," how did you react to or deal with the frustrations from others?

_____

Based on your responses to all the questions above, what would you identify as most important to you and that you tend to push for when working with others?

_____

Finally, which of these would you describe yourself as? Circle the choice that best represents you when working on your own or with others.

9. Explorer
10. Clarifier
11. Selector
12. Completer

How would you rate your own adaptability to the four learning needs?

   Not adaptable   Quite adaptable   Very adaptable

CHAPTER 4

The Learning Needs Inventory

4.1 Purpose of the Learning Needs Inventory

The Learning Needs Inventory (LNI) was developed and tested over four years. It is a reliable, robust, and valid measure that combines established research and concepts on experiential learning, work motivation, and creativity/innovation. The purpose of the LNI is to create an adaptability profile based on the strength of an individual's learning needs and to chart one's own innovative and execution capacities.

4.2 Understanding the Critiques of ELT from Research

In chapter 2, we discussed experiential learning theory (ELT), one of the most widely used concepts for leadership and management training. Organizations and educational institutions have used the Learning Styles Inventory (LSI) developed by David Kolb based on his book *Experiential Learning*. The four learning styles were a way to understand the preferred learning style when someone does something new, and from that style move through the cycle of learning.

Despite the established use of ELT and learning styles in educational and organizational settings, learning theorists and researchers have criticized the learning styles of ELT, largely stating that the ipsative (forced ranking) scoring system of the LSI is problematic, as it does not lend itself to testing and validation by statistical analysis that measures central tendency. Some researchers have also translated the ipsative scoring system to that of a scale so as to test the four styles. In the UK review of learning styles discussed in the previous chapter, some studies that used this scoring translated to a scale showed different combinations of two of the learning modes, suggesting that there are only two learning styles. These findings put into question the validity of the four learning styles, as either two or three styles emerged when the ipsative scoring system was translated into a scale and tested with analytical approaches possible for scales.

One of the motivations for developing the learning needs theory of motivation was to develop a scale to measure the learning needs underlying each learning style instead of treating the styles from a knowledge perspective, as theorized by ELT. It is hoped that this scale will demonstrate the existence of four learning styles using analytical approaches that are based on a central tendency, such as factor analysis, to test measurement models. When we translated learning styles to underlying learning needs and tested the scale, four factors emerged. We reviewed and analyzed each across four factors, identified as follows:

1. Underlying need for information
2. Underlying need for clarity
3. Underlying need for parameters
4. Underlying need for action

The LNI was also developed with work motivation theories in mind. We will now discuss these theories briefly.

4.3 Motivation Theories and Work Motivation

Motivation theories emerged in the 1960s and have not been developed much since then. Based on most of these theories, underlying these definitions are three fundamental components of motivation: *what* motivates people; *why* people behave the way they do; and *how* they align with the environment or the situation. In a recent review of motivation theories,[9] the authors extended motivation to include the situation an individual is embedded in as a factor to be considered. People are constantly interacting with the environment, and so motivation is defined as a psychological process resulting from that interaction.

Although numerous motivation theories exist, few deal with aligning with the situation individuals find themselves in, especially in a work context. Drawing from these foundational works on motivation, researchers[10] have recently identified work motivation as an area relevant to both organizational and educational contexts. It is a phenomenon that involves both intrapersonal and interpersonal dynamics around needs, values, beliefs, and goals. We extend work motivation to include alignment with situational or environmental needs, especially in the work context. A simple framework on work motivation can be depicted as shown in the diagram below.

---

[9] G. P. Latham and C. C. Pinder, "Work Motivation Theory and Research at the Dawn of the Twenty-First Century," *Annual Review of Psychology* 56 (2005): 485–516.

[10] Examples include the following: D. van Knippenberg, "Work Motivation and Performance: A Social Identity Perspective," *Applied Psychology: An International Review* 49, no. 3 (2000): 357–71; J. S. Eccles and A. Wigfield, "Motivational Beliefs, Values, and Goals," *Annual Review of Psychology* 53 (2002): 109–32; G. Latham, *Work Motivation: History, Theory, Research, and Practice* (London: Sage, 2007); L. Curral and P. Marques-Quniteiro, "Self-Leadership and Work Role Innovation: Testing a Mediation Model with Goal Orientation and Work Motivation," *Revista de Psicologia del Trabajo y de las Organizaciones* 25, no. 2 (2009): 165–76.

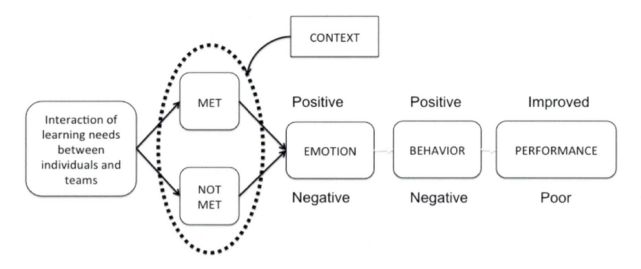

Applying this framework to the LNI, we can see that when individuals understand what motivates them and others, the interaction between them and their team or work colleagues would lead to their needs being met and hence improve performance. Being unaware or ignorant of the learning needs of others would be detrimental to effective engagement. The goal is to generate more positive emotions and behaviors, as well as increased performance, when interacting with others in organizations and educational institutions.

Our belief is that motivation and learning are intertwined, and therefore we focus on developing a measure to align with both learning and work motivation. As the LNI is a blend of learning and work motivation, it would be extremely relevant to individuals and teams, especially to achieve effective engagement in both organizational and educational settings. With the current volatile work and educational contexts, the need for individuals to develop skills to both innovate and execute is an important

> In our current volatile work environment, individuals will need to develop skills to both innovate and execute.

aspect. The LNI is especially powerful because it includes behavioral skills for developing innovation and execution in work and educational contexts.

4.4 Adaptability Profile Using the Learning Needs Inventory

The LNI report profiles a person's adaptability to changing conditions when working on projects or tasks. The diagram below shows two examples of adaptability profiles, demonstrating how unique each profile is for individuals. The profile also helps with effectively coaching individuals to develop adaptability associated with their profession, work environment, and demands.

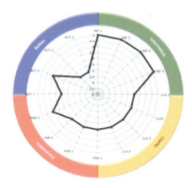

Primary Underlying Need:
Information

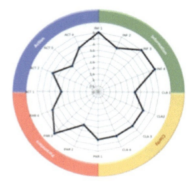

Primary Underlying Needs:
Information and Parameters

4.5 Behavioral Similarities in Creativity, Innovation, and Design

A. Creativity

Creativity has a profound effect on change at the individual, team, and organizational levels, resulting in increased engagement and performance. Leaders and managers are beginning to focus on understanding how to work within a volatile and unpredictable environment and developing skills to work with others as team members and leaders. This new organizational landscape has created a marked increase in the need to understand creativity and the creative process.

Researchers and practitioners would readily agree that organizations are constantly undergoing processes of change or development; adapting and innovating is a constant process. Research on creativity, spearheaded by Guildford in 1950,[11] has increased exponentially,[12] with concepts related to strategy, innovation, and design.

Research on creativity has focused more on the characteristics of the phenomenon itself and not much on the creative process. Existing models include a linear stage model;[13] a componential model;[14] a model focusing on subprocesses like problem solving, divergent and convergent processing, attention-demanding processing, and combination and reorganization;[15] as a highly recursive process;[16] and a dynamic instead of a linear stage model.[17] Current approaches to creativity include a four-stage model of the creative process: idea generation, development, finalization/closure, and evaluation.[18] The four-stage model presents the process from conceptualization to evaluation with capacities related to ideation, precision, project/task management, and action or completion.

---

[11] J. P. Guilford, "Creativity," *American Psychologist* 5 (1950): 444–54.

[12] F. Barron, *Creative Person and the Creative Process* (New York: Holt, Rinehart and Winson, Inc., 1969).

[13] Guilford, "Creativity," 444–54.

[14] T. M. Amabile, *Creativity in Context* (Boulder, CO: Westview, 1996).

[15] M. D. Mumford, M. I. Mobley, C. E. Uhlman, R. Reiter-Palmon, and L. M. Doares, "Process Analytic Models of Creative Capacities," *Creativity Research Journal* 9 (1991): 63–76.

[16] M. A. Runco, ed., *Problem Finding, Problem Solving, and Creativity* (Norwood, NJ: Ablex, 1994).

[17] T. I. Lubart, "Models of the Creative Process: Past, Present, and Future." *Creativity Research Journal* 13, no. 3/4 (2001): 295–308.

[18] J. E. Nemrio, "The Creative Process in Virtual Teams," *Creativity Research Journal* 14, no. 1 (2002): 69–83.

B. Innovation

In research and practice on innovation, it has been proposed that effective innovation is possible when there are individuals on a team representing all four learning styles based on ELT. As each learning style has strengths, the combination of all four would maximize those strengths and minimize any lack, which in turn makes effective innovation happen. Others have taken a more abstract view by suggesting that innovation involves latent needs, technological trends, and business needs.[19] From a skills perspective, innovation has been proposed to involve three skills: technical, creativity, and social.[20]

C. Design

Design thinking is a recent trend in organizations and educational institutions. A few models have surfaced, including phase, characteristics, and skills. Phase models are presented as having three or four phases. Three-phase models include inspiration, ideation, and implementation;[21] constructing, using, and communicating artifacts;[22] hearing, creating, and delivering;[23] and discover, define, develop, and deliver.[24] Characteristic models have been articulated as having cognitive, attitudinal, and interpersonal aspects. Finally, when framing design thinking as a set of skills, scholars have indicated that the activities associated with design thinking involve

---

[19] P. Bicen and W. H. A. Johnson, "Radical Innovation with Limited Resources in High-Turbulent Markets: The Role of Lean Innovation Capability," *Creativity & Innovation Management* 24, no. 2 (2015): 278–99.

[20] C. Lee, S. K. "Joanna," and R. Benza, "Teaching Innovation Skills: Application of Design Thinking in a Graduate Marketing Course," *Business Education Innovation Journal* 7, no. 1 (2015): 43–50.

[21] T. Brown and J. Wyatt, *Stanford Social Innovation Review* (Winter 2010): 30–35.

[22] M. Avital, R. J. Boland, and K. Lyytinen, "Introduction to Designing Information and Organizations with a Positive Lens," *Information and Organization* 19, no. 3 (2009): 153–61.

[23] T. Brown and J. Wyatt, *Stanford Social Innovation Review* (Winter 2010): 30–35.

[24] Design Council, "The Design Process: The 'Double Diamond' Design Process Model" (2004), available at http://www.designcouncil.org.uk/designprocess.

engagement. The three forms of engagement are engaging in empathy, engaging in dialogue, and engaging in collaboration.[25]

All of these models have foundations in creativity, and in reviewing these three major concepts, you would see phase models, characteristic or descriptive models, and models related to skills and behaviors. We looked at all three major concepts and focused on those related to skills and behaviors as they are framed as competencies that can be developed. Skills common to all three concepts can be summarized as ideation, evaluation or analytical skills, and implementation, collaboration, or interaction skills.

4.6 Innovation and Implementation Tendencies in the Learning Needs Inventory

Results from the LNI profile not only an individual's adaptability but also behavioral tendencies in relation to innovation and implementation. Since individuals would push the team to meet their learning needs, this push is experienced as a behavioral tendency in the work environment.

> The LNI profiles a person's adaptability and tendencies when working with innovation and implementation.

One's innovation capacity involves the combination of two needs, where one combination is the *ideation tendency* and the other combination is the *selection/synthesis tendency*. Ideation is a combination of the level of one's need for information and need for clarity. Selection/synthesis is the combination of the level of one's need for parameters and need for action.

One's implementation capacity involves combinations of the other two needs, where one combination is the *clarification tendency* and the other combination is the *action tendency*. Clarification is the combination of the level of one's need for clarity and need for parameters.

---

25 J. Benson and S. Dresdow, "Design for Thinking: Engagement in an Innovation Project," *Decision Sciences Journal of Innovative Education* 13, no. 3 (2015): 337–410.

Action is the combination of the level of one's need for action and need for information. The diagram below shows the axis of innovation and the axis of implementation and their respective combinations of learning needs.

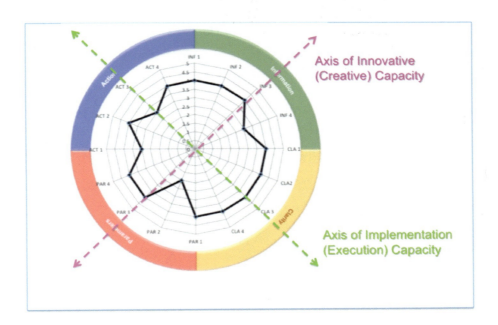

4.7 The Learning Needs Theory of Motivation

Learning, motivation, and creativity/innovation are core foci in organizational and educational contexts. Here, we treat creativity, innovation, and design as having similar behavioral characteristics, although conceptually, they are quite distinct. Considering behavior and skills, all three foci are personal attributes that are affected by a person's background and attitudes, various external

Our current global environment requires leaders have the ability to manage a diverse body of talent to push for innovative ideas, perspectives, and views in their work.

conditions, and individual learning preferences. The success of any organization in today's global environment would rely on the ability of its leaders to manage a diverse body of talent that can bring innovative ideas, perspectives, and views to their work. This is especially true for multinational companies that have operations on a global scale and employ people of different countries, ethnic and cultural backgrounds, and learning styles. This is also true in an educational environment as more students from across the globe are learning together in classroom or online settings.

The learning needs profiles show that there are fundamentally four behaviors associated with each learning need. The behavioral tendencies were discussed in chapter 3 as follows: the explorer (need for information), the clarifier (need for clarity), the selector (need for parameters), and the completer (need for action). Table 1 below describes behaviors of individuals with a predominant learning need.

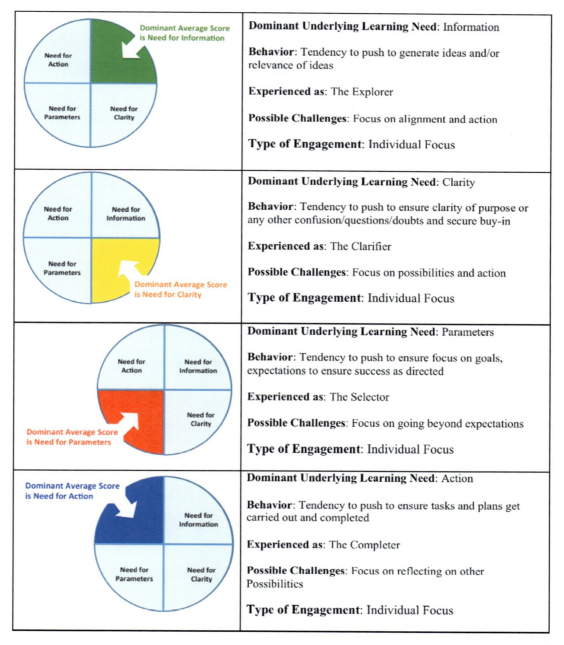

Dominant Underlying Learning Need: Information

Behavior: Tendency to push to generate ideas and/or relevance of ideas

Experienced as: The Explorer

Possible Challenges: Focus on alignment and action

Type of Engagement: Individual Focus

Dominant Underlying Learning Need: Clarity

Behavior: Tendency to push to ensure clarity of purpose or any other confusion/questions/doubts and secure buy-in

Experienced as: The Clarifier

Possible Challenges: Focus on possibilities and action

Type of Engagement: Individual Focus

Dominant Underlying Learning Need: Parameters

Behavior: Tendency to push to ensure focus on goals, expectations to ensure success as directed

Experienced as: The Selector

Possible Challenges: Focus on going beyond expectations

Type of Engagement: Individual Focus

Dominant Underlying Learning Need: Action

Behavior: Tendency to push to ensure tasks and plans get carried out and completed

Experienced as: The Completer

Possible Challenges: Focus on reflecting on other Possibilities

Type of Engagement: Individual Focus

Table 1

Unlike learning styles that identify you as having one of four styles when doing something new, the adaptability profile of the LNI takes into account our tendencies and behaviors in work settings that push us to attend to two underlying needs. Individuals push for these needs through interaction with others in work settings. Hence, not everyone ends up with one clearly dominant need. Being able to push for two needs equally (or close to equally) would give six possible combinations. Table 2 shows these combinations.

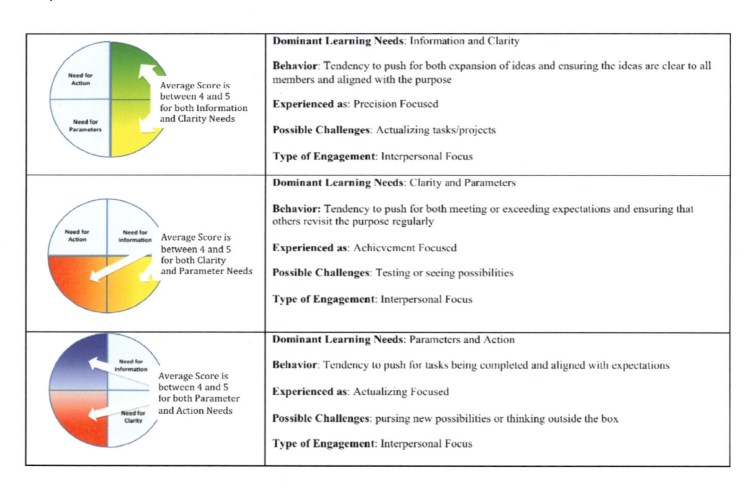

Average Score is between 4 and 5 for both Information and Clarity Needs	**Dominant Learning Needs**: Information and Clarity **Behavior**: Tendency to push for both expansion of ideas and ensuring the ideas are clear to all members and aligned with the purpose **Experienced as**: Precision Focused **Possible Challenges**: Actualizing tasks/projects **Type of Engagement**: Interpersonal Focus
Average Score is between 4 and 5 for both Clarity and Parameter Needs	**Dominant Learning Needs**: Clarity and Parameters **Behavior**: Tendency to push for both meeting or exceeding expectations and ensuring that others revisit the purpose regularly **Experienced as**: Achievement Focused **Possible Challenges**: Testing or seeing possibilities **Type of Engagement**: Interpersonal Focus
Average Score is between 4 and 5 for both Parameter and Action Needs	**Dominant Learning Needs**: Parameters and Action **Behavior**: Tendency to push for tasks being completed and aligned with expectations **Experienced as**: Actualizing Focused **Possible Challenges**: pursing new possibilities or thinking outside the box **Type of Engagement**: Interpersonal Focus

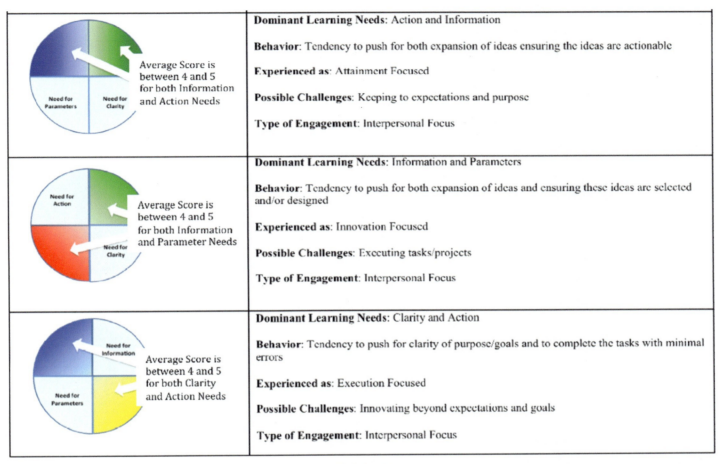

Dominant Learning Needs: Action and Information

Behavior: Tendency to push for both expansion of ideas ensuring the ideas are actionable

Experienced as: Attainment Focused

Possible Challenges: Keeping to expectations and purpose

Type of Engagement: Interpersonal Focus

Dominant Learning Needs: Information and Parameters

Behavior: Tendency to push for both expansion of ideas and ensuring these ideas are selected and/or designed

Experienced as: Innovation Focused

Possible Challenges: Executing tasks/projects

Type of Engagement: Interpersonal Focus

Dominant Learning Needs: Clarity and Action

Behavior: Tendency to push for clarity of purpose/goals and to complete the tasks with minimal errors

Experienced as: Execution Focused

Possible Challenges: Innovating beyond expectations and goals

Type of Engagement: Interpersonal Focus

Table 2

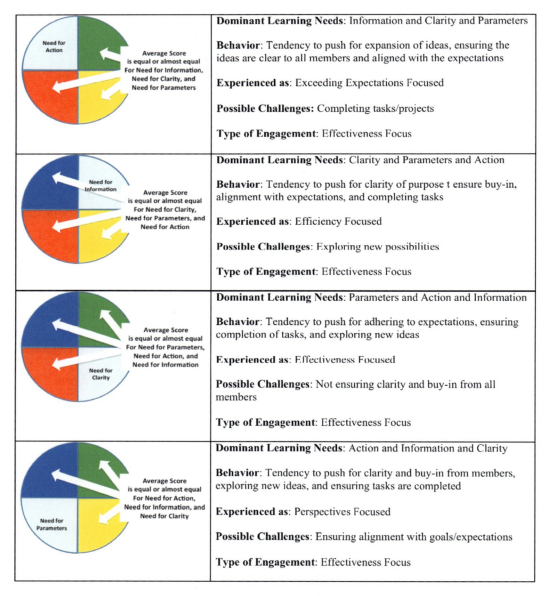

	Dominant Learning Needs: Information and Clarity and Parameters **Behavior**: Tendency to push for expansion of ideas, ensuring the ideas are clear to all members and aligned with the expectations **Experienced as**: Exceeding Expectations Focused **Possible Challenges**: Completing tasks/projects **Type of Engagement**: Effectiveness Focus
	Dominant Learning Needs: Clarity and Parameters and Action **Behavior**: Tendency to push for clarity of purpose t ensure buy-in, alignment with expectations, and completing tasks **Experienced as**: Efficiency Focused **Possible Challenges**: Exploring new possibilities **Type of Engagement**: Effectiveness Focus
	Dominant Learning Needs: Parameters and Action and Information **Behavior**: Tendency to push for adhering to expectations, ensuring completion of tasks, and exploring new ideas **Experienced as**: Effectiveness Focused **Possible Challenges**: Not ensuring clarity and buy-in from all members **Type of Engagement**: Effectiveness Focus
	Dominant Learning Needs: Action and Information and Clarity **Behavior**: Tendency to push for clarity and buy-in from members, exploring new ideas, and ensuring tasks are completed **Experienced as**: Perspectives Focused **Possible Challenges**: Ensuring alignment with goals/expectations **Type of Engagement**: Effectiveness Focus

Table 3

We have also seen individuals with three equal or almost equal learning needs. For such individuals, there are four possible combinations, as shown in Table 3.

Finally, an individual who has all four needs equal or almost equal would be someone with well-rounded adaptability. Table 4 shows this profile.

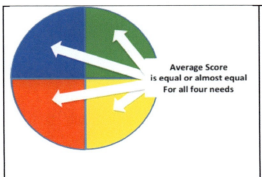

Average Score is equal or almost equal For all four needs	**Dominant Learning Needs**: Information, Clarity Parameters, and Action **Behavior**: Tendency to push for innovation and execution **Experienced as**: Engagement Focused **Possible Challenges**: Minimal **Type of Engagement**: High Impact Focus

Table 4

The learning needs theory of motivation and the LNI can be an effective applied methodology to identify an individual's adaptability profile and develop skills related to innovation and execution, which would in turn lead to effective engagement and better teamwork in organizations and educational institutions. This methodology incorporating the use of a validated and robust measure (the LNI) with coaching can help leaders, managers, and educators to improve performance, individual development, and job satisfaction due to the intrinsic link between work motivation and creativity.

4.8 Using the LNI in Organizations and Educational Institutions

In today's organizational environment, the ability of leaders and managers to develop skills to work with and lead teams is becoming highly necessary for success. As organizations become more team oriented, the critical need to understand the complexity of the team experience should not fall by the wayside. The LNI raises awareness of individuals' underlying needs and helps members in organizations and students in educational institutions develop adaptability and skills to improve their innovation

> Results from the LNI raise awareness of individuals' underlying learning needs so as to help them develop adaptability and both innovation and execution skills critical to their success and that of the organization.

and implementation. It deepens understanding of how to work with others to create generative and collaborative work relationships at the dyad and team levels.

Summary

We developed the Learning Needs Inventory (LNI) by integrating established research and concepts on experiential learning, work motivation, creativity, and innovation, and the recent work on design thinking. The purpose of the LNI is to present an adaptability profile based on an individual's learning needs and also chart innovative and execution capacities.

One's *adaptability profile* is based on the strength of each underlying learning need. The combinations of strengths of the four needs offer a more accurate profile for each individual. There are fifteen possible profiles that can help us understand how questions are framed (by others and ourselves) and how we respond to the behavior (positive and negative) of others when engaging at the individual, interpersonal, and team levels.

One's *innovation capacity* involves combinations of two needs, where one combination is the *ideation tendency* and the other is the *selection/synthesis tendency*.

One's *implementation capacity* involves combinations of the other two needs, where one combination is the *clarification tendency* and the other is the *action tendency*.

A Reflective Exercise

Reflect on a project you have worked on with others. What characteristics of the interaction in the team helped you contribute, and what characteristics hindered you from contributing to the team? Keep in mind that you are a member of both teams. In the left column, list the characteristics that help you to contribute to the team; in the right column, list the characteristics that hindered you from contributing to the team.

Characteristics that helped you contribute to the team

Characteristics that hindered you from contributing to the team

_____   _____
_____   _____
_____   _____
_____   _____
_____   _____
_____   _____

From the above two columns:

1. What themes emerged that determine your ability to interact with others on the team?

_____
_____
_____

2. What would be possible if you knew your other team members' learning needs?

_____
_____
_____

CHAPTER 5

Developing Adaptability Using the Learning Needs Inventory

5.1 The Emphasis on Developing Teamwork Skills

Experiential learning theory proposes that individuals use their preferred learning styles when doing something new. In the work environment, "something new" may be a unique project that has never been done before or coming up with ideas and methods to improve the work environment. Yet we are interacting with others or on a team on a daily basis, and so knowing our own preferred learning style may be useful but not sufficient to achieve effective engagement. As organizations and educational institutions strategize to align with the constantly

> Teamwork skills are increasingly emphasized as critical in work and educational environments.

changing environment in which they are embedded, there is a need for individuals to develop adaptability so as to constantly evolve as work and educational contexts change.

With the increasing emphasis on creativity, innovation, and design thinking, numerous methodologies have emerged. One of the strengths of the Learning Needs Inventory (LNI) is that it profiles adaptability while identifying strengths and areas to improve upon. Weaving experiential learning, work motivation, and creativity into one assessment involves significant time and effort to test, refine, and retest before arriving at the best combination of items to capture learning flexibility or adaptability.

In today's organizational and educational contexts, more and more emphasis is being placed on teamwork. Adaptability that focuses on achieving effective engagement has two aspects:

1. The ability to know what the situation calls for and to manage requirements of the project or task while also attending to the learning needs of individual team members with the need(s) to effectively work through the project/task

2. The ability to attend to innovation and implementation skills to meet or exceed expectations given

5.2 Managing Changing Goals and Expectations at the System Level and Shifting Learning Needs at the Team Level

The first aspect of being adaptive is to be able to manage changes of goals and expectations from top management while also managing the shifts of learning needs from individual team members as the project evolves. Most team leaders or project managers are focused on getting the job done in the most efficient way. Many techniques used in project management—such as Gantt charts and critical paths—ensure that projects get done in a timely and efficient manner. Yet we have heard

> Leaders who want to increase effectiveness by paying attention to the needs of team members so as to bring out the best in them must develop the sensitivity to align with what motivates each individual.

leaders mention that their job is to focus on the people (or team) and the work will get done, to the point that sometimes the team can exceed expectations. A focus on team members requires a sensitivity to ensure everyone is engaged and actively contributing to the team while working on the project.

Recent research on teams has shown that it is important to ensure everyone is engaged by paying attention to how team members connect with one another, ensuring that some members do not dominate the effort. Our own work over the past eighteen years has shown that the least effective aspect of teamwork is focusing on the task and the most effective is having team members contribute to—and more significantly, influence—the team. But how does one do that? The answer is simple but profound: by aligning with what motivates others on the team. This is where the LNI becomes important, as it combines learning, work motivation, creativity, and innovation.

As we discussed in chapter 3, our research and analysis have shown four major needs: for information, clarity, parameters, and action. Every individual has some level of need for each of these four aspects when interacting with others in a team. It is possible to quickly assess the needs of individual members by paying attention to what need they tend to push for. When a person is shut down when pushing for a need, that individual will feel unappreciated and not valued. Hence, we lose the possibility of that person engaging with the team.

We have heard of situations where someone asks for more clarity and another team member, who has a high need for action, feels that this person is holding up the progress of the team and makes statements like "I don't think that is important right now. We should move ahead." Or sometimes a person might say, "Could you stop being so difficult? We need to just get this done." Not paying attention to how members

> Paying attention to how members frame what they say can help a leader understand what motivates them and how important it is for them.

frame what they say can lead to many instances of misunderstanding. All too often, we have heard discussions like this:

"You're not listening to me!"

"Yes I am!"

"No, you're not!"

Paying attention to how members frame what they say can help a leader or other team members understand what is motivating them and how important it is for them. The more important it is, the more they will push for it or react strongly when they are not heard or their issue is not addressed.

There are two sides of this first aspect of adaptability: adapting to what is required by the situation and adapting to address the needs of individuals on the team. When considering requirements of the situation, when faced with coming up with innovative or novel ideas, it is important to obtain ideas and thoughts or to find out information to achieve the end result of an impressive novel idea. Such a situation calls for information-gathering, and so addressing members'

> Working effectively on team projects requires the skill of adapting to the requirements of the situation and the needs of the individuals on the team.

needs for information could align easily. When getting a task done quickly, the requirement would be action, and collecting information from members would not align with the situation; it might interfere with the effectiveness of getting the task done. How does one adapt to the evolving requirements of situations and still manage the four aspects of needs of the individuals?

Adapting to the needs of individual members is a high-level skill. One must be able to immediately identify the need of that individual at that point in time. Being hit with multiple different needs simultaneously while aligning with the press of the situation and managing upward requires good leadership knowledge and a good understanding of learning needs. Simultaneously handling two or all three levels (internal, situational, and external) as shown below can be done if the leader or team member is trained to quickly identify underlying needs of the individual. This is most difficult, as needs constantly change based on how members frame what they say.

The ability to quickly identify underlying needs of individuals is a high-level skill, as these needs constantly change as the work unfolds.

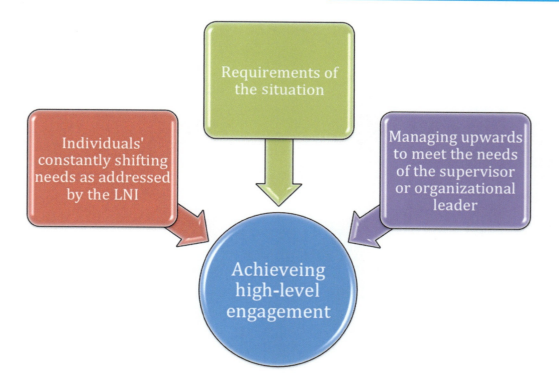

Think of this in terms of layers or levels. The foreground or immediate layer is the learning needs of individual members, and these are constantly shifting as the project unfolds. The second layer is the needs of the supervisor or organizational leader in terms of how they have framed what is required. Finally, the background layer is the requirement to contribute to the organization, as teams are embedded in the system and hence require the ability to develop systems thinking.

It is therefore important to understand how a project might shift over time to contribute to the organization effectively. Any task or project given to a team has to meet or exceed the supervisor's expectations, which may also be affected by changes in the expectations of organizational leaders as they strategize to adapt to changes from external forces. Adapting upward across three levels while managing expectations given is shown in the diagram below.

It is important to know that expectations and goals of a project or task may shift as the project unfolds to contribute effectively and align with the needs of the organization to thrive in its environment.

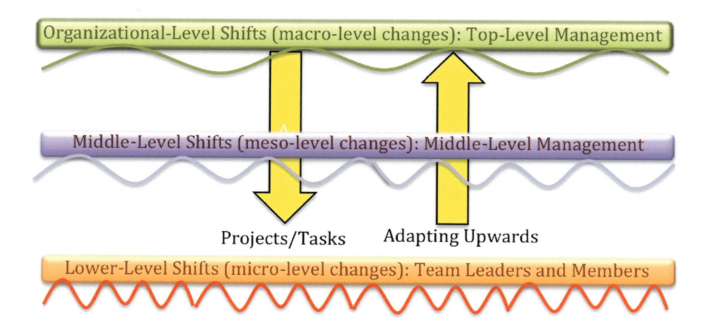

As depicted in the diagram, team leaders have to adapt to the learning needs of team members, and this requires quick recognition of their needs by listening to how they frame questions or thoughts. The team leader who knows how to address the four major aspects of learning needs will be able to ensure effective engagement of all members and be sensitive to others who may not have that knowledge. Having all members of the team take the LNI will help members know how to engage with other team members and why they might push certain aspects of the project or task, or why they might react to what others are pushing or asking for. This level of skill is what we call *adaptive managing* at the team level and *adapting upward* from the macro-micro-macro when needed.

Projects or tasks given to teams are usually related to the strategy of the organization, and team members must adapt and thrive in the environment they are embedded in. Teams are microsystems embedded in the organization. Most of the time, team leaders try to adapt to the changes in the nature or goals of the project without paying attention to the shifts of learning needs from team members as the project or task unfolds. Ability to handle or manage these changes and shifts is a major aspect of adaptability. The other is being able to ensure engagement by developing innovation and implementation skills.

> Most of the time, team leaders try to adapt to changes in the nature or goals of a project without paying attention to the shifts of underlying learning needs of individual team members as the project or task unfolds.

5.3 Attending to Innovation and Execution Tendencies at the Individual and Team Levels

The second aspect of adaptability is the ability to attend to innovation and implementation skills as a project unfolds. The LNI is designed to capture one's tendencies when it comes to the ability to innovate and the ability to implement when working on tasks or projects. The ability to innovate involves two fundamental skills: ideation and selection. We plot these tendencies for the two fundamental skills along what we call the *axis of innovation*.

> The second aspect of adaptability is the ability to develop innovation and implementation skills as a project unfolds.

5.4. The Axis of Innovation

The axis of innovation presents individuals' tendencies in their ability to focus on ideation and on synthesis/development/design. When engaging with ideation, some tend to generate as many ideas as possible (variety) or to judge the relevance of the ideas as soon as they are suggested (relevance). A person with a strong ability to engage in the ideation process can balance these tendencies. The axis of innovation (ideation) is shown in the diagram below.

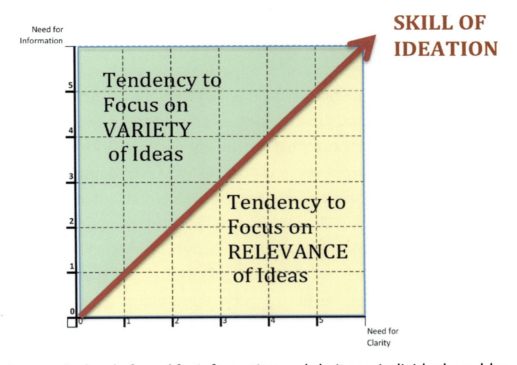

SKILL OF IDEATION

Need for Information

Tendency to Focus on VARIETY of Ideas

Tendency to Focus on RELEVANCE of Ideas

Need for Clarity

Depending on the level of need for information and clarity, an individual would end up falling into one of the colored triangular regions. If the need for information is higher than the need for clarity, the resulting point on the needs axis would fall into the green region; if the need for clarity is higher, the point would fall into the yellow region. Each region represents a tendency.

A person with a tendency for a variety of ideas (green triangle) would push to get ideas from others, get information from multiple sources, get others' perspectives on the ideas, and/or push to come up with more ideas to exceed expectations. This would result in the generation of a variety of ideas from team members. This is one way of ideation.

The second tendency is to focus on the relevance of ideas (yellow triangle). A person with this tendency will focus on determining if the ideas are relevant to the project, task, or expectations given to the team. Such a person would push to determine relevance of ideas based on how clear they are in relation to the project or task; whether the ideas can be clearly developed; whether they can be worked through systematically and thoroughly; and/or if they are clear to everyone and there is no confusion.

During the ideation process, members of a team push for variety or relevance depending on how important these needs are to them. When the team members align with these behaviors or address their concerns, they tend to be motivated and engaged. A person with the capacity to deal with the ideation process can hold the variety and relevance of ideas lightly. This individual will focus on what is or can become possible by looking at the connections or links between these ideas instead of the ideas themselves. This is a skill of ideation that balances variety and relevance, transforming ideas into possibilities.

The other aspect of the capacity to innovate is the ability to synthesize/develop/design. When engaging with selection, there are two possible tendencies. One is the ability to synthesize/develop/design emerged possibilities from the ideation process based on the parameters (expectations) given to the team. The other is to synthesize/develop/design the possibilities based on how quickly they can be put into action (feasibility). A person with a strong ability to select or synthesize can balance both expectations and feasibility. The axis of innovation (synthesis/development/design) is shown below.

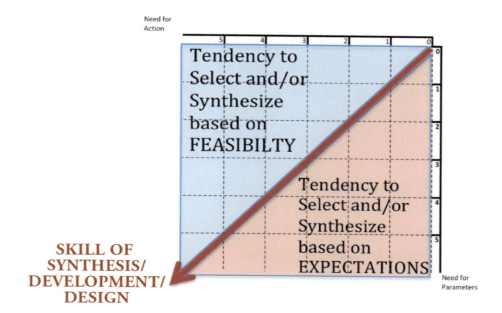

Depending on the level of need for parameters and action, an individual will fall into one of the colored triangular regions. If the need for parameters is higher than the need for action, the resulting point on the needs axis would fall into the red region; if the need for action is higher, the point would fall into the blue region. Again, these regions represent tendencies.

A person with the tendency to synthesize/develop/design based on expectations (red triangle) would push to ensure that choices from the ideation process are made based on the goals, expectations, and guidelines given to the team. If the goals, expectations, and guidelines are not given, the individual would push to obtain some criteria to work with. This would result in synthesizing/developing/designing the options that align with the goals, expectations, and guidelines given. The second tendency is to focus on the feasibility of options (blue triangle). A person with this tendency will push to synthesize/develop/design options based on how quickly they can be done.

During the synthesis/development/design of ideas and possibilities that emerge from the ideation process, members of a team will push for options that align with the expectations given or how quickly they can be done, depending on how important these needs are to them. When team members align with these behaviors or address all concerns, they tend to be motivated and engaged. A person with the capacity to deal with the synthesis/development/ design can manage the choices based on both meeting the expectations given and assessing feasibility. This individual would be able to identify critical options (i.e., those choices that meet the expectations and are feasible) so as to make wise choices that have an impact on the organization. This is a skill of synthesis/development/design that balances expectations and feasibility, focusing on choices with criticality and impact.

5.4.1. The Innovation Axis: Combinations of Ideation and Synthesis/ Development/Design Tendencies

There are five possible combinations from the tendencies as follows:

5.4.1.1   Combination #1: Variety (Ideation) and Expectations (Synthesis, Development, and Design)

A person with this combination is one who is focused on generating as many ideas as possible so as to be able to synthesize the ideas in ways that meet the given expectations or to select ideas that align with the possibility of meeting given expectations. A person with this approach will value innovation that align or meet given expectations.

5.4.1.2   Combination #2: Variety (Ideation) and Feasibility (Synthesis, Development, and Design)

A person with this combination is one who is focused on generating as many ideas as possible so as to be able to the synthesize the ideas in ways that focus on how quickly they can be carried out or to select those ideas that can be done quickly. A person with this approach will value and drive innovation that can be easily or quickly done.

5.4.1.3 Combination #2: Variety (Ideation) and Feasibility (Synthesis, Development, and Design)

A person with this combination is one who is experienced as one who evaluates and focuses on ideas that are aligned or meet the expectations given to him/her while also focusing on selecting or synthesizing these ideas to meet the expectations given. A person with this approach will value and drive innovation that align or meet expectations.

5.4.1.4 Combination #4: Relevance (Ideation) and Feasibility (Synthesis, Development, and Design)

A person with this combination is one who is experienced as one who evaluates and focuses on ideas that are aligned or meet the expectations given to him/her so as to be able to synthesize the ideas in ways that focus on how quickly they can be carried out or to select those ideas that can be done quickly. A person with this approach will value and drive innovation that meets expectations as efficiently as possible.

5.4.1.5 Combination #5: Balanced on Ideation (on or very close to the axis) and Balanced on Synthesis, Development, and Design (on or very close to the axis).

A person with this combination is one who is able to generate multiple ideas so as to be able to hold them lightly and create possibilities based on clustering ideas that emerge. When making choices, such a person would select ideas into clusters that focus on both efficiency (speed) and effectiveness (aligning with expectations). This is a person who has the skill to work with ideas so as to generate clusters of these ideas focusing on what becomes possible from these clusters that were not readily apparent when given the task or when beginning the process of working through the project's innovation phase. This person would also have the skill to select ideas/possibilities that can be implemented quickly while also paying attention to those that are important even though they may take longer to implement.

5.4.2. Axis of Implementation/Execution

The axis of implementation/execution presents tendencies to ensure clarity and action when implementing or executing projects or tasks. When engaging with clarity, some people tend to clarify any matters or issues related to the purpose, goals, and expectations of the given project or task, while others focus on clarifying any issues or matters brought up by team members so that there is no confusion about anything before moving forward. A person with a strong ability to achieve clarity can balance it in relation to the project and in relation to any other matters or issues. The axis of implementation/execution (clarity) is shown below.

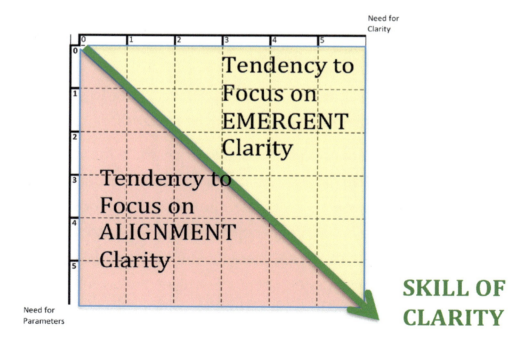

Depending on the level of need for clarity and parameters, an individual would end up falling in one of the colored triangular regions. If the need for clarity is higher than the need for parameters, the resulting point would fall into the yellow region; if the need for parameters is higher, the point would fall into the red region.

A person with a focus on ensuring clarity based on all or any issues that surface (yellow triangle) would push to ensure that every team member is clear to avoid any confusion. This tendency to ensure emergent clarity includes any issue or matter that needs to be clear even if it is not related to the given expectations, goals, or guidelines. A person with the tendency to focus on ensuring that everyone is clear on the given goals, guidelines, tasks, or expectations (red triangle) would push to ensure that everyone on the team understands what is expected when completing the project or task.

When a team engages in ensuring clarity, the two tendencies are demonstrated by behaviors from team members that push for emergent or alignment clarity. A person who has the skill to balance both aspects ensures both clarity of alignment with given expectations and team members' understanding even of matters not related to the parameters given by supervisors or faculty. The capacity to emphasize both emergent and alignment clarity provides an ability to focus on complete clarity so as to minimize any problems when transitioning to action. Lack of complete clarity could lead to reworking actions that did not go well or failed due to miscommunication or misunderstandings.

The other aspect of the capacity to implement or execute is pushing to ensure things get done (delivery and actualization). The axis of implementation/execution (delivery and actualization) has two aspects:

1. The tendency to focus on getting things done by using a checklist or following the action plan and checking things off when they get done

2. The tendency to focus on getting feedback from those affected by the action plan so as to be able to refine or adjust to meet the needs of the customer

The axis of implementation/execution (action) is shown in the figure below.

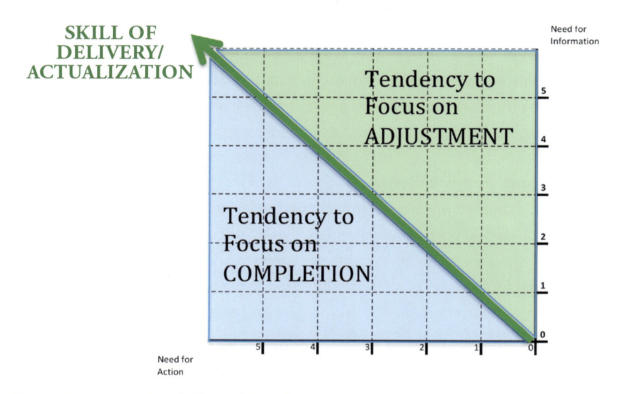

Depending on the level of need for information and action, an individual would end up falling in one of the colored triangular regions. If the need for action is higher than the need for information, the point on the needs axis would fall in the blue region; if the need for information is higher, the point would fall into the green region.

A person with a focus on completing tasks would push for getting things done as planned or use a checklist to mark tasks that are completed. The more tasks completed, the more motivated this person would be, as it aligns with a need to focus on completing tasks. However, a person with a focus on ensuring that actions done are effective would push to obtain feedback so as to adjust or refine the tasks moving forward.

Individuals who are able to focus on both completion and adjustment with equal emphasis would be able to engage effectively with team members who have either tendency. A capacity to push for both completion and adjustment enables a focus on effectiveness over efficiency.

5.4.2.1 Combination #1: Emergent (Understanding, Clarity, and Precision) and Completion (Delivery and Actualization)

A person with this combination is one who is focused on ensuring that all members of the team are not confused about any issues that are emerging or emerged that are not necessarily related to the task when discussing the goals, objectives, and expectations of the project(s) assigned. While dealing with any emergent confusion, he/she will also focus on creating a list of tasks that need to be carried out so as to ensure all tasks are completed (checked off). A person with this approach will value execution/implementation by first ensuring that there is no confusion even if it is not related to the project and to complete tasks according to a rollout plan.

5.4.2.2 Combination #2: Emergent (Understanding, Clarity, and Precision) and Adjustment (Delivery and Actualization)

A person with this combination is one who is focused on ensuring that all members of the team are not confused about any issues that are emerging or emerged that are not necessarily related to the task when discussing the goals, objectives, and expectations of the project(s) assigned. While dealing with any emergent confusion, he/she will also focus on ensuring that feedback is obtained from all stakeholders involved so as to adjust and correct any issues raised by them when implementing the tasks or roll-out plan. A person with this approach will value execution/implementation by first ensuring that there is no confusion even if it is not related to the project and to focus on refining or adjusting any implemented tasks based on feedback obtained from stakeholders

5.4.2.3   Combination #3: Alignment (Understanding, Clarity, and Precision) and Completion (Delivery and Actualization)

A person with this combination is one who is focused on ensuring that all members of the team understand and are completely clear specific to the goals, objectives, and expectations of the project(s) assigned. While dealing with any clarity of alignment, he/she will also focus on creating a list of tasks that need to be carried out so as to ensure all tasks are completed (checked off). A person with this approach will value execution/implementation by first ensuring that all members are clear about the project assigned and to complete tasks according to a rollout plan.

5.4.2.4   Combination #4: Alignment (Understanding, Clarity, and Precision) and Adjustment (Delivery and Actualization)

A person with this combination is one who is focused on ensuring that all members of the team understand and are completely clear specific to the goals, objectives, and expectations of the project(s) assigned. While dealing with clarity of alignment, he/she will also focus on ensuring that feedback is obtained from all stakeholders involved so as to adjust and correct any issues raised by them when implementing the tasks or roll-out plan. A person with this approach will value execution/implementation by first ensuring that all members are clear about the project assigned and to focus on refining or adjusting any implemented tasks based on feedback obtained from stakeholders

5.4.2.5   Combination #5: Balanced on Understanding, Clarity, and Precision (on or very close to the axis) and Balanced on Delivery and Actualization (on or very close to the axis).

A person with this combination is one who is able to ensure that there is no confusion about what is expected of the project and also answering any confusion even if the confusion is not related to the expectation of the project. When implementing tasks related to the project, he/she will be able to identify the tasks that need to be completed and checked off while simultaneously paying attention to the tasks that have been implemented that would affect stakeholders by obtaining feedback from them so as to refine or adjust such tasks to be effectively implemented into the system. This is a person who has the skill to ensure-buy in from team members by listening to any issues that may surface whether or not they are related to the expectations of the project or to improve the project itself (going beyond expectations that are collaboratively created by all team members). This person would also have the skill to ensure that tasks that tasks that need to be implemented quickly are completed while ensuring feedback has been obtained from stakeholders in the system where the project that has been implemented to effectively influence the system positively.

5.5 Using the LNI to Develop Adaptability

The LNI captures three aspects of adaptability:
1. Ability to recognize that the team is embedded in subsystems or a larger system and adapt to changes inflicted by external factors in which the organization is embedded (whether local, national, or global)
2. Ability to innovate to go beyond expectations given
3. Ability to act on tasks with a focus on effectiveness

In organizations, the ability to engage effectively with others can be significantly increased by knowing one's adaptability profile and that of one's teammates.

As the LNI has been tested and found to be robust across cultures, it can also be used in multinational corporations or global organizations. As an example, we worked with a client that had a team scattered across the globe. All team members completed the LNI to receive profiles that captured all three aspects of adaptability. Once all members completed the LNI, we coached them by phone and discussed their adaptability profile. They became more aware of their own need to push certain aspects of project work when working with others.

On the topic of innovation and execution tendencies, we were able to help team members identify their tendencies when working on projects that required innovation and also to identify specific behaviors that would help them become more skillful at ideation and selection. These specific behavioral tendencies could be identified based on the strengths of underlying motivational needs. Then the team members were able to craft new behaviors that aligned with their own strengths so as to develop more balance across the four skills related to innovation capacity. We did the same for the execution capacity. Members highlighted the value of this knowledge and skill development and decided to meet virtually to talk about their profiles and coaching session. This gave them the ability to engage more effectively with the rest of the team moving forward.

Team members first introduced themselves based on their underlying needs, and this started a great conversation. These colleagues realized why each of them would ask questions and frame issues the way they did. The conversation was lively and engaging, with each team member confirming needs and behaviors when working with one another. This knowledge increased their awareness of each other, especially when working on projects. Members further suggested ways to respond to their needs to increase feelings of value and appreciation. They also asked others to help them develop the skills from their coaching session to become more adaptable.

The above example is from a global team. Over the years, we have worked with numerous teams across different industries and across the globe using the LNI. All team members who used the LNI as part of their team training and development indicated how simple yet significant and profound this approach was for them. They were surprised to learn how easy it was to increase engagement in their teams. They acknowledged how significantly this knowledge and awareness would help them engage more effectively without reacting or blaming others. This knowledge can also help leaders and other members know how to respond to underlying motivational needs in ways that promote higher-level engagement and create an interactive space focused on valuing and appreciating others.

In the next chapter, we will dive deeper into how the LNI can be used to increase self-awareness when working with others. This knowledge is also very important for increasing levels of engagement at the interpersonal level.

Summary

In our current work environment, adaptability that focuses on achieving effective engagement has two aspects:

1. The first aspect is experienced at three levels: attending and adjusting to the constantly shifting learning needs of individual members as the project progresses (managing laterally); to the goals and expectations of one's supervisor or a leader of the organization (managing upward); and to the shifts in organizational-level needs to contribute positively to the organization (managing change).

2. The second aspect is experienced at the project level. This is the ability to attend to four innovation and four implementation tendencies of individuals as the project unfolds. The four innovation tendencies are:
    a. tendency to focus on variety of ideas
    b. tendency to focus on relevance of ideas
    c. tendency to make selections based on expectations
    d. tendency to make selections based on feasibility

3. The four execution/implementation tendencies are:
    a. tendency to focus on emergent clarity
    b. tendency to focus on alignment clarity
    c. tendency to focus on completion
    d. tendency to focus on adjustment

A Reflective Exercise

Think of a time when you (as the team/project leader) successfully managed changing expectations and goals when working on a project. What did you do to make this successful?

_____

_____

How did team members respond to your approach?

_____

_____

What challenges did you encounter, and how did you work through them?

_____

_____

How did you manage the diverse questions?

_____

_____

How did your team members respond to you focusing on individual questions?

_____

_____

What challenges did you encounter, and how did you work through them?

_____

_____

How did you motivate and work with your team members to focus on contributing to the organization (or higher system)?

_____

_____

Now think of a time when you led a team to create and implement an innovative idea. How did you manage the ideation process?

_____

_____

What was your tendency when developing ideas (variety and/or relevance)?

_____

_____

How did you manage selecting which of the ideas your team should focus on?

_____

_____

What was your tendency when selecting or designing ideas to work on (feasibility and/or expectations)?

_____

_____

Finally, think of a time when you led a team to implement a project. How did you deal with members asking for clarification on the task or any other confusion?

_____

_____

How did you manage completing or implementing the project?

_____

_____

CHAPTER 6

Achieving High-Impact Engagement at the Individual and Interpersonal Levels

6.1 Working Effectively at the Interpersonal Level

The purpose of this book is to help organizations and educational institutions enable employees and students respectively to develop skills that will enable them to effectively engage with others on a team. In the earlier chapters, we explained that effective engagement is a combination of learning, work motivation, and adaptability. We dove deeper into each of these three areas and how they can be assessed using the Learning Needs Inventory (LNI) for employee and student development.

Development in these three areas requires a reliable, valid, and robust measure to assess overall adaptive profile and innovation and execution capacities. Results from the LNI can be used to hone in on aspects that employees and students need to develop to succeed in their role in their work and educational context respectively.

The LNI provides an understanding of employees' or students' behavior and perspective by indicating what learning needs are important to them. The scores from the profile show the four aspects for each learning need. The higher the score for each aspect, the more the person would push for it, whether doing tasks individually or with a team. Each aspect of the four learning needs aligns with specific behavior and framing demonstrated by this person when working on a team. Understanding individuals' levels of learning needs will help others know why a person may be framing things a particular way or demonstrating specific behaviors when working with others.

> Understanding the learning needs of others can help us understand why people frame things the way they do and also why they might behave the way they do when we are working with them.

The higher the aspect of a learning need, the more the person would push to meet that need. When the aspects are not high, the person would not be overly concerned about these needs and so would not react if others push these aspects. If a score is very low, the individual would get frustrated when others constantly pushed for those aspects. These built-up frustrations would then result in reactions that destroy effective engagement. However, if the level of a particular aspect of learning need was high, the person would react if others did not respect those concerns or understand why they were so important.

> The strengths of each aspect of the four learning needs determine behaviors and reactions when working with others. A high level results in a person pushing for that need when working. A low level means that aspect of the need is not important, but others constantly pushing this aspect would result in frustration and destructive behaviors.

In achieving effective engagement, it is critical to understand underlying learning needs (and particularly the aspects of each of the needs) that motivate others in the team. In the work we have done, we get members in the team talking about their high-level needs and each particular aspect as part of a "getting to know your team members" session. On numerous occasions, upon hearing how they introduced themselves, others would note how aligned the results of the LNI were to people's behavior and to the strategies needed to meet those needs.

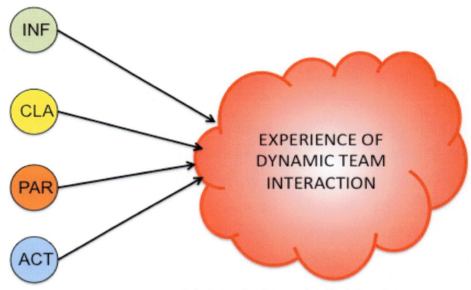

Individuals with Different Learning Needs

Listen to how individuals FRAME questions – pay attention to underlying learning needs

Effective team interaction promotes:
1. Social understanding of members
2. Understanding of purpose of the team
3. Members are able and want to contribute
4. A trusting environment so members can voice any/all their interests and concerns

6.2 Working with Learning Needs

Learning needs are central to understanding why people frame their concerns in a particular way or why they might react to others' recommendations when working together. Being able to address the learning needs of individuals during interaction requires a fast mind to immediately know the need identified and find a way to acknowledge or meet that need. Doing this would ensure higher levels of motivation and engagement.

> Learning needs are central to understanding how people frame things and how they behave when working with others. Having this knowledge and knowing how to deal or respond to these needs would ensure higher levels of motivation and engagement.

For example, if a member says, "Could we find out what others have done so we don't make the same mistakes?" it may appear that this person has the need to not make mistakes. However, the behavioral focus is on finding out what others have done. This is an example of an underlying need for information. The need could be met with answers like "That is a good idea; we can include this in our plan" or "That is a good idea; if we go into that later, would that be okay?" Such responses address the need highlighted by showing that the need has been heard and can be met immediately or after some time. The person would feel not only heard but also appreciated and acknowledged, and this would promote engagement.

> Responding positively to learning needs results in members feeling heard, appreciated, and acknowledged, thereby promoting higher levels of engagement.

> Listening to others' needs would positively affect how you engage with others and they with you.

Similarly, listening to others' needs would positively affect how you engage with others and they with you. Focusing on learning needs ensures that the people you are working with (or leading) feel valued and appreciated for what is important to them. This in turn creates a great working environment and promotes effective engagement.

All too often, we have heard of toxic relationships, toxic leaders, and work experiences that cause people to leave and find other jobs. This may be because they don't like their boss or because they feel unappreciated or undervalued. Working with learning needs can minimize such experiences and promote motivation, engagement, and retention. It also promotes healthy interaction among team members and, in turn, creates an environment where team members want to contribute to the team and positively impact the organization. We call such teams *high-impact teams* (HITs). When leaders, team leaders, and students are trained well, they will develop an ability to be sensitive to their own and others' learning needs.

> Teams that have high levels of engagement and positively impact the organization are what we call *high-impact teams* or HITs.

Different learning needs can surface at any point in time—during any interaction with others or on a team—as individuals have combinations of learning needs and hence push for different needs. The more adaptable the person is, the more that individual will be able to understand and work with the different aspects in each underlying learning need. People with a clear learning need (high on all aspects of a learning need) tend to push for that need consistently when working with others. As a team works together, members will be able to notice the different needs that individuals on the team have, making it easier to anticipate others pushing for certain needs. This level of awareness and understanding is critical to effective engagement.

> Being able to work with learning needs is an important part of leadership training and development programs.

Paying attention to learning needs also promotes motivation. When team members' needs are met, they feel valued and appreciated, and as a result display positive emotions, improved behavior, and, ultimately, higher performance. Hence, understanding, being aware, and working with learning needs is an important part of leadership training and development programs. The diagram below shows how underlying learning needs at the individual level are linked to team performance in HITs.

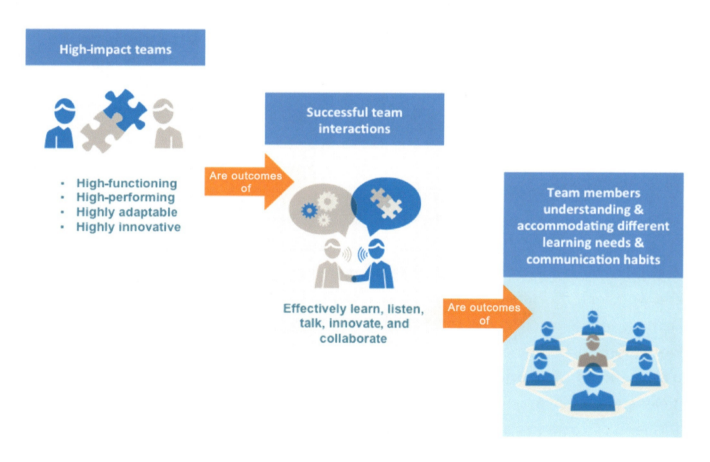

To create, lead, and develop teams to become high-impact, it is important to realize that interactions at the team level should be healthy and successful. Interactions among members center on understanding, healthy communication, active listening, and the capacity to collaborate. In order to develop healthy and successful interactions, members should understand and accommodate the different learning needs that can be displayed by tendencies to ask or frame what is important to each member. This ability in all members leads to successful team interaction, which in turn will create HITs that are high-functioning, high-performing, highly adaptable, and highly innovative.

> Interactions at the team level among members center on understanding, healthy communication, active listening, and the capacity to collaborate.

6.3 Learning Needs as a Motivational Driver for Human Systems

From a systems point of view, human beings can be considered an open system,[26] with drivers that are mainly motivation, power, influence, decision-making, and leadership. Needs theories mainly present needs as either innate or learned. When looking at underlying learning needs, such needs are mostly developed over time, just as learning styles are. We tend to use learning needs that align with what would work for us, and hence they are strong motivators when considering an individual as a human system.

Organizations have needs and groups have needs, but the needs directly involved when interacting with others are at the individual level. The learning needs that emerge in interacting with others shift faster than group or organizational needs. It is therefore important to train leaders to quickly identify individuals' needs when interacting with them. Understanding that

> Individual learning needs shifts much faster than team or organizational needs. Therefore, learning needs at the individual level are a crucial and integral part of leadership training and development.

---

[26] T. Lane, *The Living Organization: Systems of Behavior* (New York: Prager Publishers, 1989).

human systems are driven by learning needs as a motivational force enhances interaction with others and promotes engagement.

6.4 Developing Adaptability

Our discussion of the three levels of adaptability begins with the most pronounced: adapting to the different learning needs of team members during team interaction. Dealing with learning needs and relating them to the tasks or projects given by supervisors instead of focusing only on efficiency makes teamwork more effective. Truly effective teamwork requires an ability to understand that the team is embedded in a larger system and that HITs contribute to and influence that larger system. In short, team leaders are working with two levels of systems and are aware that the most effective way to lead teams is to work with the level of human systems first—that is, the underlying learning needs displayed by team members.

Paying attention to the innovation and execution capacities of the team is the next level of adaptability. The learning needs of each team member show their tendencies when working through innovation and execution. The team leader should be able to align the tendencies of individual members to maximize the potential of innovation and execution. See the diagram below as an example of the profile of tendencies of an individual.

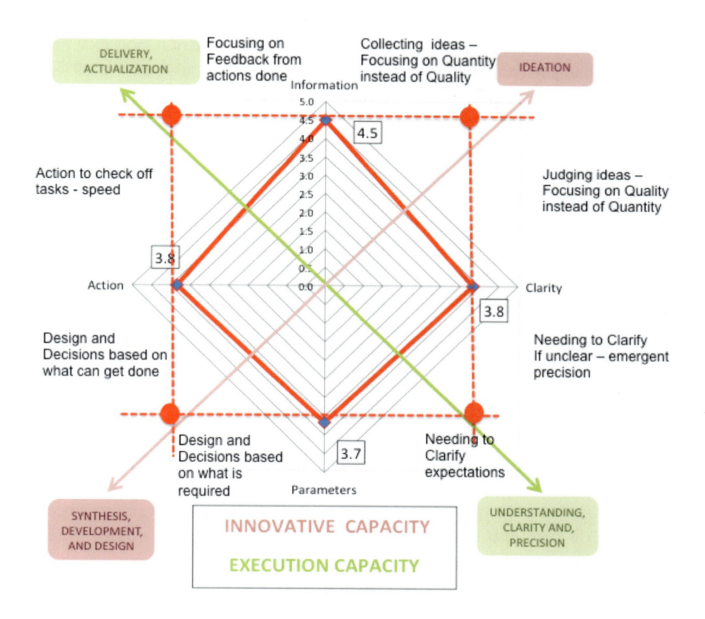

In capacity to innovate, an individual tends to push for variety during the ideation process and to select tasks that are feasible (as shown by the red dot from the kite, which is the profile from the LNI). As far as implementation or execution, this individual would focus on ensuring that no one is confused and on getting feedback to adjust and refine any initial action step that was done (again, see the resultant red dots along the implementation/execution axis).

All individuals receive a unique profile so that they can be aware of their tendencies when innovating or implementing. Knowing every team member's profile would be very helpful for determining the team's strengths and whether members need to develop any of these tendencies to move their red dot to be on the axis of innovation and the axis of implementation/execution. This would facilitate individual development as part of the coaching process.

> Individuals have their own unique innovation and execution tendencies. Improving one's skill to innovate and execute would be an effective part of individual and/or executive coaching.

Based on the profiles of individual team members, the team leader should also be able to determine how to develop team members so as to achieve the highest possible level of capacity to innovate and execute. For example, if most of the members are driven by information, ideation would tend to become the generation of a variety of ideas but lack the ability to focus on the relevance of ideas. The team leader might choose to encourage some members to develop the capacity to push for relevance so the team can achieve both variety and relevance during the ideation process. This applies to all eight tendencies related to innovation and execution. Knowing the profiles of each team member allows the leader to increase the team's capacity for innovation and execution.

Effective engagement begins at the individual level by addressing what is important to individuals as they work together on tasks or projects. Leaders and team leaders should be trained to work at this level as a critical first step to understand how to work with others and help them engage effectively. Although most project management programs focus on ways to get things done, this is equally (if not more) important when leading others. When individuals feel valued, heard, and appreciated, they will tend to display behaviors of influence, which can be very helpful in teamwork.

> When individuals feel valued, heard, and appreciated, they will tend to display behaviors that increase the team's effectiveness.

In our research and practice at the team level, we have found that the most powerful dimension of teamwork is power and influence. When team members believe they are able to exert power and influence in their team, they assess the team as performing well, they feel satisfied being team members, and they experience higher levels of psychological safety. This is one major way in which understanding and working with learning needs will promote adaptability, innovation, and effective execution—all benefits of effective engagement when working with others.

Summary

1. Understanding the learning needs of others can help us understand why people frame things the way they do and also why they might behave the way they do when working as part of a team.

2. The level or strengths of each aspect of the four learning needs determines behaviors and reactions when working with others.

3. Having knowledge of individuals' learning needs and knowing how to deal or respond to these needs ensures higher levels of motivation and engagement.

4. Teams with high levels of engagement that positively impact the organization are what we call *high-impact teams* or HITs.

5. Understanding and working with learning needs should be included in leadership training and development programs.

6. Leadership training and development programs should include individual coaching to help leaders develop adaptability and improve their capacities to innovate and execute.

A Reflective Exercise

In this short exercise, you can test your skill at listening for underlying needs. The statements were taken from chapter 3, so you can identify if you got them right. Only check back after you have completed this exercise to determine how many of the items you got correct.

	Framing of statement or question	Underlying need	Appropriate response to meet underlying need
Example	"Could we address why we are doing this project? I am still unsure …"	Clarity	"I am glad you raised this. Let me tell you what I know …"
1.	"Can we revisit our goals so as to verify that they are aligned with the goals given to us?"		
2.	"I feel like we are pushing this fast and not thinking it through systematically."		
3.	"Can we just move ahead and proceed with the next task?"		
4.	"Anyone else have other points of view?"		
5.	"I'd rather work on the urgent tasks so we can get those out of the way first."		

6.	"I need to understand what is expected of us and why."		
7.	"Could we use the internet to see what information is out there?"		
8.	"We need to ensure we have at least some criteria and expectations given to us."		

Now think of a time when you achieved high-level engagement with your team members. What techniques or concepts did you use?

_____

_____

_____

What are your own current practices?

_____

_____

_____

Considering what you have read and learned from this book, what would you do differently now to achieve high-impact engagement in your team?

_____

_____

_____

CHAPTER 7

The Utility of the Learning Needs Inventory in Organizations and Educational Institutions

7.1 Linking Leadership, Team Leadership, and Team Membership

Organizations have spent billions of dollars developing individuals, but very few focus on linking these training programs to team leadership or how to be an effective team member. Teamwork has become a crucial part of organization design where teams exist or are created across all levels. The ability to understand individuals and to know how to motivate and work effectively with them is very much needed in organizations. A program that would help support and provide methods to meet this need is important, especially when it links leadership, team leadership, and team membership.

> Training and development programs that focus on the individual, interpersonal, and team levels are critical for developing high-impact engagement and success within the work environment.

7.2 Fundamental Team Structure in Organizations

Across the globe, with the increasingly complex and volatile work environments, organizations are recognizing the importance of developing leaders and employees to increase internal capacity to innovate and enhance performance. A major shift in structural design to meet this need is to incorporate teams across all levels of organizations. In the team design of organizations, usually a team leader is a team member of another team higher up in the organization, and there are links of this sort across all levels. Such a design allows teams to contribute and/or influence organizational performance and innovation. Currently, most teams are structured and designed to complete tasks effectively, and the recent emergence of design and innovation approaches is pushing this further to include the ability for team members to develop such skills. The Learning Needs Inventory (LNI) focuses on developing adaptability and both innovation and execution capacities as the foundation for effective teamwork in organizations. The diagram below represents this structure.

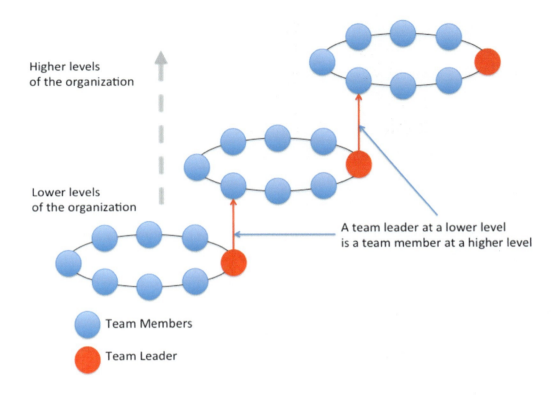

Higher levels
of the organization

Lower levels
of the organization

A team leader at a lower level
is a team member at a higher level

Team Members

Team Leader

As mentioned in chapter 1, a study conducted in 2012 involving 10,640 projects from 200 companies in thirty countries found that only 2.5 percent of companies fulfilled 100 percent of their projects.[27] A recent study in 2016[28] indicated that organizations all over the world are transitioning to a team-oriented design, thereby creating not only teams but networks of teams. This Deloitte study showed that of the countries surveyed, companies across the globe that rated the need to move to a team-oriented design as important or very important ranged from

[27] B. Hardy-Vallee, "The Cost of Bad Project Management," *Gallup Business Journal*, February 7, 2012, http://news.gallup.com/businessjournal/152429/Cost-Bad-Project-Management.aspx.

[28] T. McDowell, D. Agarwal, D. Miller, T. Okamoto, and T. Page, "Organizational Design: The Rise of Teams," Deloitte Insights, February 29, 2016, https://www2.deloitte.com/insights/us/en/focus/human-capital-trends/2016/organizational-models-network-of-teams.html.

95 percent in Asia and Africa; 90 percent in North America; 92 percent in Latin America; 93 percent in the Middle East; 92 percent in Western Europe; 91 percent in Southeast Asia; and from 88-87 percent in Central and Eastern Europe, Nordic countries, and Oceania. It is therefore no question that our future organizations are going to need exceptional team leaders and members.

However, as can be seen from the above diagram, team leaders are also team members in the basic team structure of such organizations. Hence, it is critical that we focus our attention on developing both team leadership and team membership skills so as to meet this need based on team-oriented designs as the fundamental organizational structure. The complex nature of such structures implies that organizational members could be members of a few teams and also leaders of other teams, such as project teams and ad hoc teams. Based on the diagram, team leaders must know how to work with team members, as well as work as a team member on a higher-level team. This link requires team leaders to function equally effectively as team members.

> Leadership training and development programs should include team leadership and team membership skills to function effectively in an organization.

7.3 Using the LNI for Leadership Training, Coaching, and Development

The LNI supports this need by training team leaders to adapt to the diverse learning needs of individuals (which may also shift as the team continues working together) and simultaneously to develop a better understanding of other team members and the team leader in other teams they may be a part of. A

> Due to the team-oriented structure across levels in an organization, training programs that are most effective involve team leadership and team membership knowledge and skill development, as these are better suited to the needs and operational design of the organization.

program focusing on individuals' learning needs will help team leaders develop both leadership and membership skills. When equipped with such knowledge and skills in identifying and working with learning needs, leaders can support high-impact engagement at the team and organizational levels. Due to the nature of team-oriented structures across levels in an organization, most organizational outcomes—whether project goals or key performance indicators—are tied to teams and not individuals. Thus a program that involves training in team leadership and membership is much better suited to the needs and operational design of today's organizations.

Over the past decade, we have used the LNI with multiple organizations, both for-profit and nonprofit. What was truly helpful for leaders was getting all team members to take the LNI and engage one-on-one with a certified coach (who we call an individual-level development architect). Upon completion of the individual coaching sessions, the team would meet to introduce themselves and their learning needs so that other team members could both understand and respond positively to each member when working on projects or developing ideas for the organization.

7.4 Using the LNI as a Launchpad for Team Training, Coaching, and Development

Since the development of the LNI, we have used it in numerous organizations worldwide. We have worked with for-profit, nonprofit, multinational companies, and companies in other countries. We have used the LNI across national cultures (e.g., China, Latin America, USA, Europe, and Africa); organizations from different industries; and educational institutions. The LNI has also been used with top leadership teams to identify a balance of strengths and contributing

> Teams whose members took the LNI shifted from being task-oriented to focusing on the team's ability to contribute to the larger system.

capacity of individual team members. We have also used the LNI as part of individual training and development to both strengthen individuals on the team and bring more balance. Due to the simple but profound nature of our learning needs theory of motivation, organizational members who have taken the LNI were astonished at how much they got to know about themselves and others, both from an adaptability and a capacities perspective.

Examples of comments and feedback we received are statements such as "It is unbelievable how the LNI has helped me focus more on others," "I have worked with this team for quite a while and having the LNI made me understand more about each member bringing us much closer," "I have been told by my manager that I need to learn how to work with others for me to become effective in higher level management. This session taught me that listening to others is the first step to working with people. Listening in a way that understands what motivates them and not listening to solve a program or complete a task," "This is so impressive as it helps me become so much more connected with others. This could apply to our everyday lives!" "I have never thought of listening to engage and not listening to solve or act. This session has taught me so much more than I ever imagined!" "This is beyond management and change. This is about understanding people's motivations when they engage at work."

Our experience working with teams in organizations has shown a significant shift from task completion to high-impact engagement. Creating a team development program in organizations that begins with individual members' assessments of their underlying needs using the LNI builds a solid foundation of training and development at the team level using the work context of teams within their organizations. What is most significant is the immediate shift in focus from tasks to contributing to the team and larger system.

7.5 Evidence-Based Training and Development

In 2011, more than $156 billion was pumped into training programs, most of which focus on developing individuals' leadership and supervisory skills.[29] Although companies are becoming more team oriented structurally, few programs focus on developing teams in their actual work environment—although numerous offsite team-building programs exist. From a 2014 review of numerous scholarly, practitioner, and online sources—including very recent articles—the authors mention that it is quite evident that very few team training programs focus on developing teams in their organizational context and even fewer provide evidence-based training.[30]

> Very few team training programs focus on developing teams in their work context, and even fewer are evidence-based.

> Our approach is to develop a methodology focused on developing solid research-based tools that have shown high reliability and validity nationally and globally so as to be able to design evidence-based training at both the individual and team levels.

Quite a few programs at the individual level are evidence based, but hardly any for team training and development. Our approach is to develop a methodology focused on solid research-based tools that have shown high reliability and validity nationally and globally so as to be able to design evidence-based training at both the individual and team levels. The LNI is one such tool. It was developed to provide evidence-based training and

---

[29] L. Miller, "ASTD 2012 State of the Industry Report: Organisations Continue to Invest in Workplace Learning," *American Society for Training and Development* (2012): 42–8.

[30] S. Lancaster and L. D. Milia, "Organisational Support for Employee Learning: An Employee Perspective," *European Journal of Training and Development* 38, no. 7 (2014): 642–57.

development programs at the individual level and serve as a launchpad for effective evidence-based team-level training and development programs.

7.6 Using the LNI for Assessment of Learning in Educational Institutions

The LNI is a useful tool for educational institutions to utilize when students are put into work, action learning, and project teams. Once these teams are formed, we have introduced the LNI so that members can get to know the underlying needs of other members as well as their own needs and engage in the process of innovation and execution. Awareness of individual learning needs and capacities to innovate and execute transforms the way students engage in a team while developing team-related skills that are critical to educational programs and prepare students to enter the work environment able to lead and be effective team members.

The Graduate Management Admissions Council, in its 2006 Corporate Recruiters Survey Report, further supports the need for teamwork skills from graduates. According to the report, 38 percent of recruiting organizations surveyed state that "soft skills" and "teamwork skills" are extremely important when hiring an MBA graduate into an organization. This need to develop teamwork skills in students has permeated undergraduate and graduate programs in numerous fields.[31]

> The need to develop teamwork skills in students has permeated undergraduate and graduate programs in numerous fields in educational institutions.

Based on years of work in using the LNI in educational settings, we are confident in it as a foundational requirement for developing teamwork skills. It is a reliable and valid way to positively and quickly transform the current task-oriented approach to one that is focused on the ability to work with diverse members effectively and promote high-impact engagement.

---

[31] E. Raes, E. Kyndt, S. Decuyper, P. Van de Bosse, and F. Dochy, "An Exploratory Study of Group Development and Team Learning," *Human Resource Development Quarterly* 26, no. 1 (2015): 5–30.

Another reason for the use of the LNI in educational contexts is the possibility of tracking the development of adaptability and capacities as part of student learning outcomes that has become central to academic assessment at the student, program, and institutional levels. As the focus of the LNI is to develop learning flexibility over time, entry and exit assessments of students enrolled in courses can provide concrete evidence of learning and development beyond anecdotal evidence.

In phase 1 of achieving high-impact engagement, we have focused on individual and interpersonal aspects and how the LNI can be used to help individuals become aware of their underlying learning needs and identify others' learning needs when working on projects or tasks. The LNI profiles adaptability and both innovative and execution capacities. When leadership, executive, or team training programs start with developing individual and interpersonal awareness, a richer and more effective program is possible, especially when the next phase is to link this to team-level quality of engagement and the capacities of teams to innovate and execute effectively. This combination leads to high-impact engagement at the team level and ultimately the ability of teams to contribute positively to organizational success and thrive in the work environment. In the next part of this book, we will focus on phase 2 of achieving high-impact engagement.

Summary

1. Having training and development programs that focus on the individual, interpersonal, and team levels is critical for employee engagement and leadership, leading to high-impact engagement and success within the work environment.

2. Leadership training and development programs should include team leadership and membership skills to enable employees to function effectively in an organization.

3. Due to the team-oriented structure across levels in an organization, training programs that are most effective involve team leadership and membership knowledge and skill development.

4. Teams whose members took the LNI shifted from being task oriented to focusing on the team's ability to contribute to the larger system.

5. Very few team training programs focus on developing teams in their work context, and even fewer provide evidence-based programs.

6. The need to develop teamwork skills in students has permeated undergraduate and graduate programs in numerous fields in educational institutions.

A Reflective Exercise

Reflect on your experience leading or working in teams.

1. How would you describe the difference between leadership and team leadership?

Leadership	Team Leadership

2. Have you attended training programs that start with the individual and move on to interpersonal and team-level coaching and development? If yes, what aspects helped you to be a better team leader or team member? If no, what competencies or skills would you have liked to focus on in such programs?

_____

_____

_____

3. Of all the teams you are currently involved in, how many teams are you a leader of and how many are you a member of?

Number of teams of which you are a leader	Number of teams of which you are a member

Phase 2

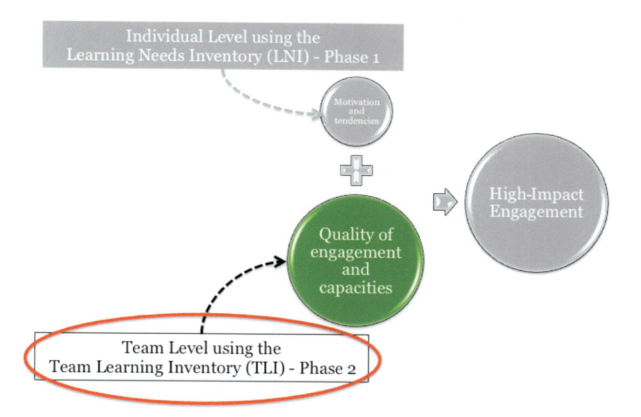

Individual Level using the
Learning Needs Inventory (LNI) - Phase 1

Motivation
and
tendencies

Quality of
engagement
and
capacities

High-Impact
Engagement

Team Level using the
Team Learning Inventory (TLI) - Phase 2

Team Level

1. Diving deeper into measuring the quality of team engagement
2. Identifying the innovation and execution capacities of a team in its work context

CHAPTER 8

Teams: The Force That Drives Effectiveness

8.1 The Ability to Influence Organizational Performance

Based on the rise of teamwork in organizations, being able to lead teams or work effectively in teams is critical. It requires the ability to develop high-impact engagement in ways that allows members to contribute and influence organizational performance. It certainly matters if we are to influence teams, organizations, or larger systems in ways that increase energy and drive to ensure evolution and success.

8.2 Teams Are the Foundation of Organizational Growth and Success

Teams. The word has become part of our way of life, whether in professional or educational settings. Undoubtedly, teams have become our primary approach to complete projects or assignments in organizations.[32] The fundamental shift toward a team-oriented organizational environment has created a push to incorporate team skills training or team development programs as an integral part of human resource development.[33] We also see a trend in educational institutions focusing on teamwork in their curriculum so that graduates can enter the team-oriented work world and succeed. This trend indicates that teams are no longer just a part of organizational structure or design but form the very soil in which an organization grows and flourishes.

> The team-oriented design in organizational structure indicates that teams form the very soil in which an organization grows, innovates, adapts, and flourishes.

8.3 The Overlapping Roles of Team Leader and Member in a Team Structure across Levels in Organizations

Most of us are team leaders, team members, or both. We are involved in multiple teams in both our organizational and educational lives. The trend is to have organizational work done at the team level because more can be achieved by teams instead of individuals doing the work alone. Teams can provide more ideas, more capacity, more innovation, and faster execution than a single individual. This is a major reason for teams becoming a driving force of organizational life. The need to have skills associated

> Teams can provide more ideas, more capacity, more innovation, and faster execution when compared to a single individual.

---

[32] B. Hardy-Vallee, "The Cost of Bad Project Management," *Gallup Business Journal*, February 7, 2012, http://news.gallup.com/businessjournal/152429/Cost-Bad-Project-Management.aspx.

[33] S. Lancaster and L. D. Milia, "Organisational Support for Employee Learning: An Employee Perspective," *European Journal of Training and Development* 38, no. 7 (2014): 642–57.

with teamwork has inspired many educational programs (undergraduate, graduate, and executive) to focus on team projects to help students learn about teamwork and develop leadership and membership skills.

8.4 Team Training Should Be Designed to Develop Teams within Their Work Context

Usually when we are put into teams—whether in organizations or educational institutions—we are given a task or project to complete and expectations or goals to meet. On the surface, it appears that teams are designed to get things done, so it should be relatively easy to accomplish tasks and expectations. However, both practitioners and scholars have found that teamwork is far more complex than just accomplishing tasks or goals. Training programs should be designed and delivered in a way that helps teams to thrive in their work or educational contexts.

Some team-level training programs offer offsite team-building but only very few focus on developing teams in their actual work context, while even fewer provide evidence-based team training and development programs. Furthermore, most team training programs and project-management courses dissect task and goals to ensure successful completion of the tasks assigned.

8.5 Team Training and Development Relevant to Today's Environment

We live in a world where needs assessments and methodologies to help teams achieve higher functioning and higher performance are becoming essential. Such approaches help each unique team improve its capacity to innovate and execute. The need to design and deliver programs that promote

> This book is the culmination of over eighteen years of research and practice. It is also based on our own experiences as organizational leaders in our professional lives.

successful teamwork and to show evidence of the impact of such training programs was a driving force in our creation of a valid, reliable, and robust system to meet this need. This book is a result of the work we have done over the past eighteen years as leaders in professional organizations, as well educators and consultants of organizational development and change. It is the culmination of research and practice focusing on the experience of teamwork as a human system that involves adaptability, underlying motivational needs, innovation, and execution capacities. It has been scientifically shown to improve teamwork at the individual, team, and organizational levels.

We hope that this book will open your mind to the fact that the most important aspect of teamwork is not outcomes or expectations but rather the experience we go through while working in these teams. As individuals, we can clearly articulate experiences that were great and others that were frustrating and even toxic. We all belong to teams that span this continuum of positive and negative experiences, but we are not usually taught skills to shape our experiences when working in teams. Instead, we respond based on our own experiences. That being the case, it cannot be the individual who is to blame but rather the collective experience of the team. In this book, we show how we as educators, leaders, and consultants can shape team experiences to help teams function and perform well and to drive effectiveness at the team and organizational levels. We call such teams *high-impact teams* or HITs.

Before we discuss how to create and sustain HITs in organizations, we will discuss the types of teams we encounter in organizations, healthcare, and educational institutions.

8.6 Teams in Organizations, Healthcare, and Educational Institutions

Despite the trend of organizations becoming more team-structured, few programs focus on developing teams in the actual work environment, although numerous offsite team-building programs exist. Studies show that very few leadership and team-development programs focus on developing teams in their organizational context, with even fewer providing evidence-based training for teams.[34]

Even though organizations are moving to incorporate teams as part of their structure—as teams can offer greater adaptability, productivity, and creativity than individuals; provide more complex, innovative, and comprehensive solutions to solve organizational problems; and have a positive impact on organizational outcomes[35]—leading, managing, and being a member of teams can be complex, with team experiences varying from rewarding to extremely frustrating. In essence, the positive contribution of teams to organization-level outcomes is countered by how difficult it is for organizational members to work in teams effectively.

> The positive contribution of teams to organizational-level outcomes is countered by the inherent difficulty experienced when teams try to focus on interacting effectively.

> Various types of teams exist in organizations, and we all find ourselves in a few of these.

When we look at an organization through the lens of its functioning or operating modes, teams immediately surface as the fundamental building blocks. From the top echelon to the frontline employees, organizational members find themselves in at least one team. Although numerous types of teams exist in organizations, we will discuss a few familiar teams that exist most organizations.

---

[34] K. Kruse, "The Need for 'Evidence-Based Training,'" *Chief Learning Officer*, September, 17, 2004; S. Lancaster and L. D. Milia, "Organisational Support for Employee Learning: An Employee Perspective," *European Journal of Training and Development* 38, no. 7 (2014): 642–57.

[35] E. Sundstrom, K. P. DeMeuse, and D. Furrell, "Work Teams: Applications and Effectiveness," *American Psychologist* 45 (1990): 120–33.

8.7 Top Management Teams

Top management teams (TMTs) are usually made up of board members—who come from diverse backgrounds—and senior leaders in an organization. Senior leaders form the top tier of teams within an organization. Usually the team members would include the chief executive officer, other members from the C-suite (e.g., chief operating officer, chief financial officer, chief information officer, chief learning officer), or other senior vice presidents, usually including the senior vice presidents of human resources, finance, marketing, sales, general counsel, corporate development, strategy, and operations. Some may also include those with international roles or regional functions. An organization's TMT is usually made up of interdisciplinary functions focusing on the organization's mission, vision, direction, and overall business outcomes, such as profits and other matters commonly reflected in an organization's annual report.

Although there is a strong focus on organizational outcomes, TMTs have to be able to work extremely well and thrive on healthy interaction and trust. Usually at this level, team members are faced with relentless pressure from competitors, scrutiny from stakeholders, and uncertainty regarding the strategic vision of the firm. Task and relational conflict at this level can significantly affect the functioning of such a team. To prevent such detrimental effects, team members have to engage in frequent interactions so as to develop the right atmosphere, keep misperceptions at a minimum, and establish shared understanding. Also, at this level, team members have their own executive coaches to help them succeed in their role. The team may include a corporate ombudsman to deal with conflict within the team and the organization.

8.8 Departmental or Functional Teams

A typical departmental or functional team includes a leader and team members who have expertise within a particular function (e.g., human resources, finance, accounting).

As an example, the human resources functional team would be led by the senior VP of human resources, with team members having expertise in subareas like compensation, employee relations, benefits, training and development, organizational development, employment, and records. The team's focus would be to meet departmental objectives, which may include being involved with and servicing other departments. These teams may not be as cross-functional as TMTs, but members have to work extremely well with one another.

8.9 Project Teams

Project teams vary greatly between organizations and departments. They are usually focused on a specific task or project and can be found in all levels of an organization. Project teams may be cross-functional and sometimes even self-managed. Teams may be tasked with quality control, work improvement, or specific projects for the organization, department, or even a client. Usually, they have the authority to implement their own recommendations, or they may present their findings and recommendations (that may include organizational reform or introduction of new products or technology) to their managers or other organizational leaders.

8.10 Ad Hoc Teams

Ad hoc teams are short-term teams formed to work on a task. The team members can vary from functional to cross-functional. Sometimes the task involves using a specific approach (e.g., analysis, benchmarking, and research). On occasion, organizational members may not see themselves as a team under such conditions but rather as a group of people splitting up work to complete a task or simply contributing to a certain part of a project, after which their commitment is over. Ad hoc teams can be so rampant in organizations that an organization member could be on two, three, or more such teams simultaneously.

8.11 Self-Managed Teams

Self-managed teams are self-contained work units that can occur throughout an organization. They may function like project teams or ad hoc teams but are usually tasked with producing a product or providing a service. In such teams, members are more invested in each other's function or role and may have to learn all of the jobs and tasks performed by the team as a whole. Members may also be required to be cross-trained and therefore have the ability to switch roles or job tasks and even exist in a shared leadership environment (i.e., taking turns playing the role of leader). Such teams manage their own administration, including scheduling, ordering materials, managing boundaries between the team and other stakeholders, staffing, job or role assignments, and achieving (and on occasion also defining) the team's goals, purpose, and objectives.

All of these teams can be found in large or publicly held local businesses, small to medium enterprises, or multinational or transnational companies. Some of these teams can also be found in family-owned business. Although the labels and purposes of these teams can vary vastly, they all have embedded lived experiences that can be rewarding or challenging depending on how these compare to the experiences members would like to have (ideal experiences). Further, each team in every organization has a unique lived experience that is always compared to members' own unique ideal experiences.

In this book, we show that when a team's actual lived experience is close to the members' ideal, it can thrive and succeed. Organizations that realize this are trying to incorporate coaching at the team level, but most team training programs do not have a valid or robust method for coaching teams that parallels the applicability and robustness of executive coaching at the individual level.

8.12 Teams in Healthcare

The current health care context has evolved to become extremely complex and chaotic. Given the multiple stakeholders and interests, some scholars have tried to look at health care as a complex adaptive system, while others who highlight the diverse cultures existing simultaneously would frame it as more of a chaotic system. With the Institute of Medicine highlighting the importance of interprofessional education and teamwork, scholars and practitioners are beginning to focus on the need to incorporate the design of interprofessional teams, but very few have dived into techniques or methods that help such teams develop.

One approach that has been used in the different health-focused schools in universities (e.g., medicine, nursing, dentistry, and social work) is to develop interprofessional education across these schools. Students are put into interprofessional teams to help them understand different perspectives, education, and approaches to patient-centered care through patient simulation exercises or community projects. Although helpful, programs focusing on the development of interprofessional teams are difficult to create. Yet in hospital systems, the need to develop interprofessional teams is becoming more critical with the emphasis on patient-centered care.

At a 2017 health care conference organized by the Frances Bolton School of Nursing, Case Western Reserve University, at which one of us participated in a panel discussion, participants highlighted that effective frontline teams (at the point where patients or their families first encounter care) are critical to quality and safety and to the success of hospital systems. Frontline teams are interprofessional in nature, and developing these teams to be effective is another indication of the need for effective teamwork. More research and practice must be done to help such interprofessional teams succeed, as their membership is usually fluid in nature (i.e., the professions may be the same but different individuals take part for each profession depending on the availability of those individuals). However, when considering the experience of teamwork, even teams with fluid membership can be coached to be more effective when these experiences are aggregated, averaged, and used as data for training and development. The experience of working in teams will be discussed in more detail in the next chapter.

8.13 Teams in Educational Institutions

Business and management schools are realizing the importance of having robust team-focused courses as part of undergraduate or graduate programs. Top-ranked business schools are looking into creating programs to focus on including both ethics and teamwork, while others focus on keeping students in teams throughout their education. Educational-institution gatekeepers, such as the Association to Advance Collegiate Schools of Business, and publications that rank educational programs, such as the *Wall Street Journal* and *US News and World Report*, are finding that team-focused programs are critical for educational success. Undergraduate and graduate programs are beginning to develop courses such as Action Learning[36] to parallel organizational trends and focus on helping students develop more "soft skills" and project management skills. Aligned with this finding is research by the Graduate Management Admissions Council that shows 38 percent of recruiting organizations surveyed think that strong soft skills are extremely important when hiring an MBA student into an organization. Project management skills are also attractive to recruiters.

Despite such a spectrum of teams in organizations, health care, and educational institutions, and with the many team training and development programs, numerous teams are still not able to achieve the level required to effectively contribute to the system in which they are embedded. We put forward that one major reason why this is not working as anticipated is because most of our team programs are focused on how to get things done efficiently instead of creating effective team experiences to facilitate and develop high-impact teams. In the next chapter, we dive deeper into the experience of teamwork in these diverse contexts.

---

[36] R. W. Revans, *The Origin and Growth of Action Learning* (Brickley, UK: Chartwell-Bratt, 1982).

Summary

1. The team-oriented focus is indicative of the fact that teams are no longer just part of organizational structure or design but form the very soil that helps an organization grow, innovate, adapt, and flourish.
2. Most of us are team leaders, team members, or both in multiple teams in our organizational and educational lives.
3. Teams are beneficial and a driving force in the work environment. They can provide more ideas, more capacity, more innovation, and faster execution compared to an individual working alone.
4. Practitioners and scholars put forward that teamwork is far more complex than just accomplishing tasks or goals.
5. In our current work environment, the need to design and deliver programs that promote successful teamwork and to also show evidence of the impact of such training programs is increasingly emphasized.
6. The positive contribution of teams to organizational-level outcomes is countered by the inherent difficulty experienced when teams try to focus on interacting effectively.
7. Various types of teams exist in organizations, and we all find ourselves on a few of these.
8. Teams have become ubiquitous. One can find teams across all levels of an organization and also in diverse work environments. Teamwork has also become an emphasis in educational institutions.
9. Although teams may have different characteristics, designs, tasks, functions, and modes of operation, the experience of teams ranges from great to extremely frustrating.
10. Teams that are cross-functional (in organizations) and interprofessional (in health care) are becoming necessary, as they enable members to collaboratively contribute more effectively to the larger system where multiple roles and functions exist.

Documenting Your Team Experience

Your current organization or educational institution:

_____

How many teams do you belong to? _____

How many teams do you lead? _____

Based on the diverse types of team in organizations, health care, and/or educational institutions, what types of teams have you been a part of (also indicate how many teams in each type)?

Type of Team	Number of Which You Are a Member	Number of Which You Are a Leader
Top Managements Teams		
Departmental or Functional Teams		
Project Teams		
Ad Hoc Teams		
Self-Managed Teams		
Interprofessional Teams		
Student Teams		

What would you estimate as the amount of time you spend working in teams (percentage in relation to your work/educational programs (circle one)?

15%	30%	45%	60%	75%	90%

CHAPTER 9

The Experience of Working in Teams

9.1 The Complexity of the Team Experience

From our experience working in organizations, conducting training programs for organizations, and being faculty members at educational institutions, common difficulties highlighted by team members in organizational and educational settings revolve more around team interaction than team outcomes. When we look at training programs for project management, LEAN initiatives, quality control, or work improvement, most of the focus of the training is on developing skills to manage and complete projects, which in turn is aimed at generating better organizational outcomes. Yet our experiences with such teams indicate complexities in managing non-task-related interactions as well, which usually are not incorporated in training programs. As a result,

> Some leaders in organizations and faculty in educational institutions try to help teams focus on tasks, believing that the teams will be more productive.

team leaders tend to push teams to concentrate on and contribute to tasks that increase organizational performance with the idea that this will focus the team on being more productive.

9.2 The Desire to Lead Effective Teams

When leaders are asked if they would love to have effective teams, they immediately respond in the affirmative; but when asked further how they as team leaders can contribute to creating self-sustaining successful teams, they respond that they see their role as managing the team's boundaries. As we engaged with executives in the numerous programs we have conducted with US, multinational, and transnational corporations, the need to be able to lead and manage teams is highlighted as critical to success in their jobs. Some managers wish they had some feedback or "sensing" mechanism in place for teams so that they can be proactive instead of waiting until a crisis emerges, at which point it may be too late, and interpersonal relationships, trust, and individual reputations will have been severely negatively affected. They also express interest in developing an understanding of the diverse aspects of team interaction and to develop the skills to create the right (and unique) environment for each team to succeed.

> Leaders in organizations have expressed the desire to create, lead, and sustain effective teams.

9.3 Reactions to the Team Experience from Leaders and Members

Reactions that leaders encountered from team members (or expressed as their own) are most frequently focused on interaction-related issues. The following are examples of team reactions:

> Reactions and thoughts team members have or baggage they carry from previous team interactions can significantly affect their experience of working in teams.

- "Not another team meeting!"
- "It is amazing how many team meetings we have."
- "Can we not just focus on getting the job done?"
- "I am tired of having to carry most of the load for the team projects all the time. This time I am going to let others carry the load so that they know what it is like."
- "Why is it that other team members cannot work with the same effectiveness and efficiency that I can?"
- "I think these team meetings are just a waste of time so that others can feel like they are contributing."
- "I don't really like this particular team member."
- "I am doing most of the work while others have more time on their hands and manage so well that it comes across that they are also working hard. Why can't others see through that?"
- "No one wants to deal with the issues that we have in the team."
- "Why can't we share responsibilities?"
- "I don't know why the team leader does not deal with the 'problem' person in the team."
- "I feel like I cannot voice what I really feel, as I don't feel safe on this team."
- "No one really seems to want my opinions or suggestions. I know my ideas are important, but the others are too focused on just getting what is asked of them. I know that there is a better way, but no one wants to listen. If only they would spend time to really listen and not talk so much!"
- "What I don't understand is the other team I used to work with was so wonderful. We could accept challenging projects and actually enjoy each meeting we had. I wish this team could be like the other one I was on."

When you look at these, think about how often we experience such feedback from those we work with (or in our own thoughts). Although some comments seem trivial and even petty, they are real to those members and would certainly influence their experience of working with the team.

9.4 Using Aspects of Team Interaction to Describe the Team Experience

Even as organizational members discuss with us how complex and frustrating it can be to lead or work in a team, the main frustrations are not usually caused by outcomes. Instead, working with multiple personalities, different learning styles, laziness, or lack of commitment from team members are identified as the most difficult issues. A common request we receive from consultants, trainers, and faculty is to help them develop team leadership and membership skills, which include effective communication strategies.

In educational institutions, most students find themselves being placed in teams and left to work through their team issues as long as they deliver their projects or end products on time and at an acceptable quality. However, when students are asked to identify what constitutes a great team experience, they highlight aspects of team interaction that include trust, relating to others, safety, and other social-emotional aspects of team interaction more than task-oriented interaction.

Similar issues are raised when organizational members are asked to identify exceptional team experiences in team development or other executive education programs. Some organizational leaders mention that they feel their job as team leader involves the following:

- acting as a filter to protect members from having too much unnecessary information that may distract them from the task or cause more confusion
- providing members with clear direction and purpose so that the team can function effectively
- getting the best people on the team so that the job can be done well and efficiently

Most executives in training programs we conducted agree that if a team is functioning well and thriving, the outcome can only be great and the experience rewarding. They also agree that the key competency as a team leader is to have a high level of team awareness, which would mean having the knowledge and skill to provide teams with a system to promote team-directed learning and development that would help them move toward healthy or good team experiences.

When we probe further into what constitutes a good team experience, teams in educational institutions and organizations realize that at the core of an effective and efficient team is how faculty or team leaders help the team understand the task at hand while also offering to help team members know how to work together and interact. Most of these aspects of team interaction are embedded in the lived experience of the team.

9.5 The Continuum of Team Experience

Apart from our experience as consultants and trainers for organizations, our interest in understanding the experience of team interaction was also triggered by the number of graduate students coming to us with problems they had in their teams. As faculty members teaching undergraduate and graduate students in a management school, we are exposed to the managers and leaders of the future while also being privileged to have the ability to see, guide, and help students in a team setting. In class sessions or during coaching sessions, most students mention that faculty members "throw" them in a team and expect them to be able to function well and produce results.

> Team experiences in the work environment involve relational, task, leadership, and environmental aspects.

Similarly, most organizational members find themselves being placed in teams and left to work through their team issues as long as they deliver their projects or end products on time and at an acceptable quality. However, when we probe further to ask team members to identify what constitutes a great team experience and a poor one, they highlight aspects that include relationships, tasks, leadership, and a healthy work environment. Most of these aspects of team interaction are embedded in the lived experience of the team based on the quality of their interactions on the task-relational continuum. Some of the comments team leaders and members make are shown below.

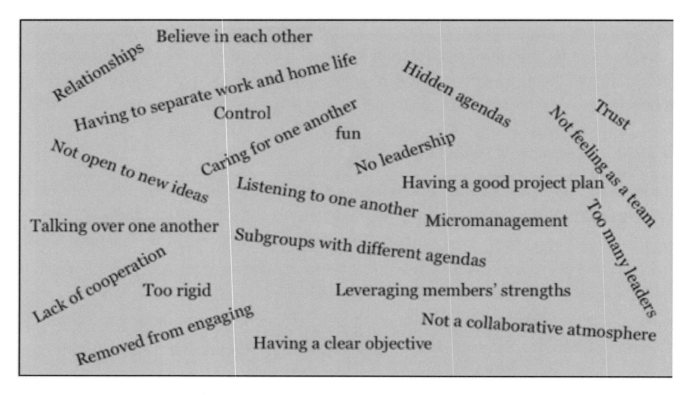

"Good" and "not so good" experiences in teams: Some responses from team leaders
and team members

Whether we like it or not, being on a team is now very much a part of organizational life. In fact, we are expected to have the skills to work with teams and even to lead or manage teams. Regardless of our level in an organization setting, we find ourselves on at least one and occasionally three or even four teams at one time. Some we enjoy being a part of, while in others we may encounter great difficulty.

At the end of this chapter, we provide you with an exercise to assess your own team experiences. This exercise can be used for the team or teams that you lead or are a member of to assess their past or present experience. Such an exercise would provide you with some initial but good insights into team experiences in your organization.

In the next chapter, we present research and findings that highlight the critical aspects of team interaction leading to the quality of team engagement and team experiences. Our research has shown that these aspects are consistent across local, national, multinational, and global teams as well as across organizations, industries, and educational institutions.

Summary

1. Some leaders in organizations and faculty in educational institutions try to help teams focus on tasks, believing that the teams will be more productive.
2. Leaders in organizations have expressed the desire to create, lead, and sustain effective teams.
3. Reactions and thoughts team members have or baggage they carry from previous interactions with their team or other teams can significantly affect the experience of working in teams.
4. These reactions, thoughts, and baggage can be identified by listening to how members frame statements or questions when engaging with others.
5. Our experience of teamwork varies from team to team but usually spans the continuum from great to extremely frustrating.
6. Team experiences in the work environment involve relational, task, leadership, and environmental aspects.

Team Experience Assessment

On this side of the page, write down the characteristics of a team you were a part of where you had a very positive experience and would certainly work with this team again.	On this side of the page, write down the characteristics of a team you were a part of where you had a very negative experience and would not like to work with this team again.
_____	_____
_____	_____
_____	_____
_____	_____
_____	_____
_____	_____
_____	_____
_____	_____
_____	_____
_____	_____
_____	_____
_____	_____
_____	_____
_____	_____
_____	_____
_____	_____
_____	_____
_____	_____
_____	_____
_____	_____

Based on your reflections from the above exercise:

1. What are the characteristics of the interactions that made them great experiences?

_____

_____

_____

_____

_____

2. What causes some team experiences to be positive and effective while others are not?

_____

_____

_____

_____

_____

3. What are the critical aspects of team interaction?

_____

_____

_____

_____

_____

CHAPTER 10

The Nature of Team Interaction: Critical Aspects That Contribute to the Experience of Teamwork

10.1 The Need to Understand Team Interaction

Team research since the turn of the century has highlighted the need to focus on team interaction[37] so as to gain a better understanding of how teams evolve through emergent states.[38] As theories of change have evolved, so has the science of teamwork and team development. Inspired by this, we leveraged our own experiences of teamwork in

> Theories of team development evolved over time and were largely based the change theories that existed in the hard sciences at that time.

---

[37] A. P. Hare, "Roles, Relationships, and Groups in Organizations: Some Conclusions and Recommendations," *Small Group Research* 34, no. 2 (2003): 123–54.

[38] J. A. Colquitt and C. L. Jackson, "Justice in Teams: The Context Sensitivity of Justice Rules across Individual and Team Contexts," *Journal of Applied Social Psychology* 38, no. 4 (2006): 868–99.

organizations, management/business schools, and interprofessional teams in health care; our consulting practice on team leadership and team coaching, learning, and development with diverse organizations ranging from local to multinational companies; and our knowledge and skills in research to develop a measuring and mapping system that could capture the experience of team interaction. After two years of testing our measurement and structural models at the local, national, and global levels, we have developed a robust, reliable, and valid scale that captures team interaction.

Drawing from existing theories on learning, creativity, and team research, we delved deeper into how the experience of teamwork can be captured, mapped, and leveraged for effective team coaching and development. Being senior executive master coaches ourselves, we wanted to create an effective team-level 360-degree assessment capturing the quality of team engagement, teams' innovation and execution capacity, and the experiences of those who work with the team as clients or supervisors. We embarked on this journey at the turn of the century and tested the measure for reliability, validity, and robustness across nations and cultures.

Our findings show that team interaction involves four major dimensions:

1. Diverging or nontask
2. Converging or task
3. Power and influence
4. Openness

See appendix B for details of the process, methods, and analytical approach we used. In this chapter, we will discuss each of these dimensions by first defining the dimension and then revealing which aspects of teamwork are most affected. We then describe any aspects of the dimension.

> The four major dimensions of team interaction contributing to the experience of teamwork are diverging; converging; power and influence; and openness.

10.2 The Dimensions of Team Interaction

10.2.1. Diverging

The diverging or nontask dimension is defined as the extent to which a team is engaged in valuing one another, connecting with one another, and allowing individuals to freely relate to one another. This interaction is not task- or purpose-focused. The diverging dimension of team interaction can be identified as those interactions that focus on nontask aspects that affect the socio-emotional dynamics in a team. Such interactions can impact the following:

- trust in the team, as it is shaped by members' values, attitudes, moods, emotions, and personal experiences
- understanding and working or managing diversity in the team (e.g., learning styles, nationalities, cultures, experiences, and gender)
- social integration (i.e., members' attraction to the group, satisfaction with other members of the team, and social interaction among team members), group cohesiveness, member satisfaction, person-group fit, and team commitment
- team bonding, which reflects feelings that members hold toward each other and the team going well beyond trust to reflect a strong sense of rapport and a desire to stay together, even beyond the current context
- ability to manage conflict experienced in a team setting
- development of skills to promote interpersonal understanding and interpersonal sensitivity

Within this dimension are five aspects of team interaction:

1. *Engagement*—When engaged, members feel involved emotionally, dealing with feelings and reactions and being open and receptive to new experiences. In this aspect of team interaction, high engagement is experienced when all members are actively involved

in team discussions—generating ideas, working through conflict, and managing diversity—and are committed to any behavioral expectations (norms). This leads to the development of trust.

2. *Active listening*—Members engaged in active listening take time to listen and look at all sides of an issue before acting. Where a high level of active listening is experienced, members become aware of the perspectives of other members. People often tell us that we are not listening to them even though we heard what they were saying. We may have heard what they *said* but not what they were *trying to say*. Restating what members say and allowing them to further express or reframe/restate their point is a very good way to develop active listening skills. This aspect, when developed, would lead to members feeling valued and appreciated, which in turn develops trust, team bonding, and understanding the basis and generation of conflict from others' perspectives. This aspect also helps team members achieve higher levels of interpersonal sensitivity, which in turn promotes higher levels of member satisfaction and social integration.

3. *Individuality*—Members should be free to be unique individuals in the team, act independently, and share their own unique life experiences. Teams are unique entities. They have to work as a unit while also realizing that each member of the team is unique. Each team member brings individual experience, knowledge, skills, interests, and expertise. Team members should not be clones or clone-like. Although this seems unlikely, we have come across numerous cases where members expected others to behave just like them. When individuality is high, members are able to share their perspectives, views, and opinions based on their past experiences. It is important to realize that all members of a team have their own experiences (good, neutral, or bad) from other teams they have been a part of. It is important to also acknowledge the diverse experiences (another aspect of managing diversity), knowledge, expertise, traits,

and abilities of team members—and allow them to voice related matters and contribute to the team. Bringing individuals into the team is a critical component of team interaction and highlights the uniqueness of their actual and desired team interaction.

4. *Relationality*—Members wish to be connected to other members through acting and agreeing on issues. They try to fit into the group. Where there are high levels of relationality, members care and are concerned for each other, not as fellow members completing a task but rather as individuals who are members of the team. Establishing behavioral norms all team members agree on and are committed to would enhance relationality. Discussions in which team members need to come to an agreement or consensus are interactions that highlight relationality in teams. Being able to connect with team members requires an ability to recognize and hold one's own perspective; recognize, value, and relate to the perspectives of others; and adjust one's own view to align with that of others. Relationality promotes team bonding and trust.

5. *Solidarity*—Members want to be seen as equals or peers. Where solidarity is high, members are conscious of the team and concerned about the team—in essence, team-minded. Such interactions focus on the identity of the team, and members work together to create high-point experiences with the intent to generate more positive team experiences. Solidarity promotes team identity, values, social integration, and team bonding.

10.2.2. Converging

A team's converging or task interaction is defined as the extent to which the team engages in decisions and is driven by agendas or directions related to the task or purpose. The converging dimension is experienced as helping the team accomplish a task, goal, or objective. This dimension of team interaction can impact the following:

- team potency (team members' collective belief that they can be effective)
- task-related conflict (such as social loafing, perceptions of indispensability, and scapegoating)
- understanding of team roles

Within this dimension are three aspects of team interaction.

1. *Understanding*—The understanding aspect includes the rationalizing and evaluating of ideas or issues that are raised in relation to the team's task or purpose. Such interactions are focused on understanding the task at hand or clarifying the purpose of the team. Many team leaders assume that members know the purpose of the team, but on most occasions, they realize that not all members share the same understanding. Members should engage in interaction to clarify the goal or purpose of the team, as they tend to behave in a manner that aligns with their perception of that goal or purpose. Developing a shared goal or vision that is clear to all members is critical to team potency and role assignments, and would help clear up any task-related conflict that might arise.

2. *Action*—The action aspect is defined as the desire to get things done or to try things out rather than merely thinking about them. In such interactions, members tend to be results oriented and practical, with a focus on doing or acting on issues or matters so as to complete the task at hand. Getting things done helps members feel that the team is capable and effective. Completing tasks efficiently is the focus of such interactions. High levels of action in the team increase team potency.

3. *Planning*—The planning aspect describes the desire for members to function effectively to complete tasks or projects by developing agendas and including time constraints imposed by members of the team or given to them by managers, leaders, or clients beyond the bounds of the team. Such interactions are deliberate and task-focused so as to allow the team to function in accordance with a planned agenda with a thorough

understanding of critical paths, roles, processes, and project management. Focusing on such interactions would allow team members to develop into system thinkers and project managers. This aspect of team interaction leads to higher levels of team potency and better management and expectations of team roles.

10.2.3. Power and Influence

A team's power and influence is defined as the extent to which members of the team have equal ability and opportunity to influence and contribute to the team's purpose, goals, and tasks. With a high level of this dimension, the team does not depend on a strong single leader; instead, members can contribute to exceed the leader's expectations and requirements.

When a team is young, usually members would expect to have strong leadership from the legitimate leader of the team. As a team matures, the nature of leadership should evolve and be shared, with members feeling they can influence the team's purpose and goals while also contributing in ways that go beyond completing assigned tasks. This is the most powerful dimension in the experience of team interaction, based on statistical analysis. Therefore, even a small gap in this dimension could have a strong effect on members' perception of team performance, satisfaction, and psychological safety.

The power and influence dimension can impact the following:

- team impact (a team's contribution to the organization)
- team innovation (a team's ability to innovate and execute)
- team performance based on contribution from each member
- team-member satisfaction (the ability to contribute and influence the team, which causes members to feel empowered and satisfied)
- shared leadership
- the psychological safety of the team

- team potency
- team efficacy

10.2.4. Openness

A team's openness is defined as the extent to which members focus on issues or ideas that are of interest or concern to individual members or the group as a whole. This dimension is focused on how safe and accepted team members feel, in terms of promoting behaviors that are inclusive at the individual and team levels. This dimension is indicated by the ability and freedom of team members to return to previously discussed issues, to stay with issues, or to discuss issues or matters that are important to them—even those that lead to tangential discussions. This dimension focuses on the freedom of individuals to voice opinions or speak up on issues that are important to them without being ridiculed; brushed away as insignificant, unimportant, or irrelevant; judged; or evaluated. It is the extent to which members are able to highlight and focus on issues or ideas that are of interest or concern to individual members or the group as a whole. The openness dimension is the second-most-significant dimension of team interaction and promotes member satisfaction, psychological safety, and group performance.

The openness dimension can impact the following:

- team psychological safety
- member satisfaction
- relationships and connectedness
- trust

Summary

1. Team interaction has been identified as critical to understanding team experience in the workplace.

2. In our work across the United States as well as in other countries and cultures, we have identified four major dimensions of team interaction that are reliable, valid, and robust.

3. The four major dimensions and their subsumed aspects (where indicated) are:

   a. Diverging
      - engagement
      - active listening
      - individuality
      - relationality
      - solidarity

   b. Converging
      - understanding
      - action
      - planning

   c. Power and influence

   d. Openness

Reflecting on the Four Dimensions of Team Interaction from Your Team Experience

Based on your past (or current) experience leading and being a team member, identify when you have experienced the four dimensions of team interaction:

The Diverging Dimension

On this side of the page, write down *positive* experiences of this dimension.	On this side of the page, write down *negative* experiences of this dimension.
_____ _____ _____ _____ _____ _____	_____ _____ _____ _____ _____ _____
How did these experiences affect teamwork? _____ _____ _____	How did these experiences affect teamwork? _____ _____ _____

The Converging Dimension

On this side of the page, write down *positive* experiences of this dimension.	On this side of the page, write down *negative* experiences of this dimension.
_____ _____ _____	_____ _____ _____

_____
_____
_____
_____

How did these experiences affect teamwork?	How did these experiences affect teamwork?

_____
_____
_____

The Power and Influence Dimension

On this side of the page, write down _positive_ experiences of this dimension.	On this side of the page, write down _negative_ experiences of this dimension.

_____
_____
_____
_____
_____
_____

How did these experiences affect teamwork?	How did these experiences affect teamwork?

_____
_____
_____

The Openness Dimension

On this side of the page, write down *positive* experiences of this dimension.	On this side of the page, write down *negative* experiences of this dimension.
How did these experiences affect teamwork?	How did these experiences affect teamwork?

CHAPTER 11

The Team Learning Inventory

11.1 Purpose of the Team Learning Inventory

The Team Learning Inventory (TLI) was first developed in 2005 and has been tested globally in numerous industries. It has been shown to be reliable, valid, and robust across countries and cultures. The TLI was developed based on experiential learning, conversational learning, team research and practice, and creativity/innovation. We present the details of our research methods and analytical approach in appendix B. The purpose of the TLI is to present a team's quality of engagement (or the experience of team interaction); its capacity for innovation and execution; and the experiences

> The purpose of the TLI is to provide a team with a 360-degree assessment. Internal assessment includes quality of engagement, innovation and execution capacities, and outcomes. The external assessment includes how supervisors and clients experience the team.

of others (clients and supervisors) who work with the team. The TLI provides a 360-degree feedback system to create high-impact teams.

11.2 Expanding Experiential Learning to Conversational Learning

In chapter 2, we discussed experiential learning theory (ELT), one of the most widely used concepts for leadership and management training. Organizations and educational institutions have used the Learning Styles Inventory and its four styles in leadership and management training and development programs. In 2002, Kolb and colleagues developed the theory of conversational learning[39] with the intent of taking ELT to the team level. Conversational learning was developed using qualitative methods and analysis but was not empirically tested in a quantitative way to support the theoretical framework.

In essence, the theory of conversational learning is conceptualized as having five dialectical poles:

1. Apprehension (APP) ↔ Comprehension (COM)

    Central to the theory of experiential learning, apprehension and comprehension represent the dialectically related ways in which we grasp knowledge. Integrated knowing occurs through equally embracing these ways. This can be stated as the emotional-conceptual dialectic. Integrated knowing is experienced as a strong grasp of both concrete and abstract knowledge.

2. Intention (INT) ↔ Extension (EXT)

    Also central to the theory of experiential learning, intention and extension represent the dialectically related ways in which we use knowledge when equally embracing these

---

[39] A. C. Baker, P. J. Jensen, and D. A. Kolb, eds., *Conversational Learning: An Experiential Approach to Knowledge Creation* (Westport CT: Quorum Books, 2002).

two ways. This can be stated as the reflective-action dialectic. This integrated use of knowledge is experienced as being results oriented and practical.

3. Individuality (IND) ↔ Relationality (REL)

Individuality is experienced as the freedom of members to be unique individuals in the team, with the ability to act independently and share their own unique life experiences. Relationality is experienced as the desire to be connected to other team members through the acting and agreeing on issues.

4. Status (STA) ↔ Solidarity (SOL)

Status is experienced as having the need for leadership to guide, decide, and help others learn. There is a clear status hierarchy in the team. Solidarity is experienced as the desire to be equals or peers, where leadership is shared. Members learn from one another, make decisions as a team, and have strong personal relationships with each other

5. Discursive (DIS) ↔ Recursive (REC)

Discourse is experienced as the desire of members to move on based on agendas and time constraints either imposed by members or given to them by those outside the team. Recourse is experienced as the tendency to return to previously discussed issues (or to stay with issues) that capture the attention of team members.

11.3 Overview of Team Research and Practice

Team research began blossoming in the 1950s when working in teams flourished in the military, organizations, and educational institutions. As more organizations incorporate a team-oriented design as part of their structure due to the increased impact of teams over individuals, researchers have aligned with this trend to focus more on teamwork in organizations and educational institutions to develop a better understanding of how teams function or operate and to help teams thrive.

This effort over the years has resulted in multiple approaches to teamwork. Some argue that team life is so complex that it would be best to peel it apart and zoom into the various aspects, while others state that team life needs to be understood as a whole instead of dissected. We will discuss this bifurcated approach to teamwork to show the numerous perspectives embedded in each path and trace how team research has evolved over the years.

> Over the years, the approach to teamwork has become bifurcated. Some zoom into specific aspects of teamwork, while others argue that we have to understand teamwork as a whole.

11.4 Zooming In on Various Aspects of Teamwork

Researchers who consider teamwork to be highly complex and difficult to study as a whole suggest that it is best examined by zooming in on its various aspects. This has given us a better understanding of these aspects. Broadly, those that have emerged can be clustered into three categories: antecedents (or inputs), process, and outcomes. The diagram below shows some aspects that have emerged from this approach to understanding teamwork.

1. Antecedents (Inputs)	2. Processes	3. Outcomes
Team Design Team Diversity Team Roles Task Characteristics Reward Systems	Team Dynamics Task ← → Relational Aspects Team Conflict Team Learning Team Communication Decision-Making Interpersonal Understanding Team Functioning	Team Performance Member Satisfaction Psychological Safety

More specifically, early team research and leadership studies established that interactions between team members and between leaders and followers exist in a task-relational continuum.[40] As team research evolved, researchers began to peel apart this continuum and look at the diverse variables embedded therein.[41] Other researchers delved into how the nature of a task affects a team's functioning or the level of its productivity. Team process research is perhaps the most diverse, ranging from group dynamics (including intra- and inter-level processes) to task and relational aspects of teamwork that might include project management.

Most research that focuses on these diverse aspects of team processes is also linked to team outcomes so as to demonstrate the impact of these processes on outcomes or deliverables. Team outcomes as used in some team research include performance, member satisfaction, and psychological safety, apart from actual performance measures linked to organizational goals.

As can be seen in the input-process-output diagram, peeling apart the various aspects of teamwork can provide an in-depth understanding of these variables, but it does not really help teams as a whole to be more effective. Other team researchers therefore claim that we have to understand teams as a whole, especially with the emergence of new scientific theories such as systems, complexity, and chaos theory.

11.5 Looking at Teamwork as a Whole

From a holistic perspective, researchers have proposed moving away from the input-process-output approach to include a feedback loop from output back to input, creating a dynamic system. Such a concept suggests that teams are constantly evolving from one state to another. The diagram below shows this perspective.

---

[40] D. Cartwright and A. Zander, *Group Dynamics*, 3rd ed. (Oxford: Harper and Row, 1968).

[41] Team research that zooms into various aspects of teamwork can be found in appendix B of this book: "Developing the Team Learning Inventory (TLI)—Design and Analyses."

Although this approach does propose that teams are constantly evolving, it is based on how outputs affect new inputs. This shift of input-output-new input is based on the perspective that team development or growth is based on how the outputs affect the new inputs to the team. Although there is value in this approach, the states of a team are not directly related to output-input.

At the turn of the century, researchers began to propose that teams are complex dynamic systems, aligning with more recent scientific theories of change, such as chaos, complexity, and complex adaptive systems. Researchers[42] who support this view of teams as complex dynamic systems also suggest that team development is not linear but rather based on changing from one state to another based on how the team interacts. This emerging trend in conceptual frameworks presented by researchers does not have much empirical support. One suggestion for understanding this perspective is that team research should dive deeper into the concept of team interaction and how this helps us understand how teams evolve from one state to another.[43] The diagram below depicts some of the complexities and the diverse research streams involved in understanding teamwork.

---

[42] Team research that focuses on the holistic nature of teamwork can be found in appendix B of this book: "Developing the Team Learning Inventory (TLI)—Design and Analyses."

[43] A. P. Hare, "Roles, Relationships, and Groups in Organizations: Some Conclusions and Recommendations," *Small Group Research* 34, no. 2 (2003): 123–54; J. A. Colquitt and C. L. Jackson, "Justice in Teams: The Context Sensitivity of Justice Rules across Individual and Team Contexts," *Journal of Applied Social Psychology* 38, no. 4 (2006): 868–99.

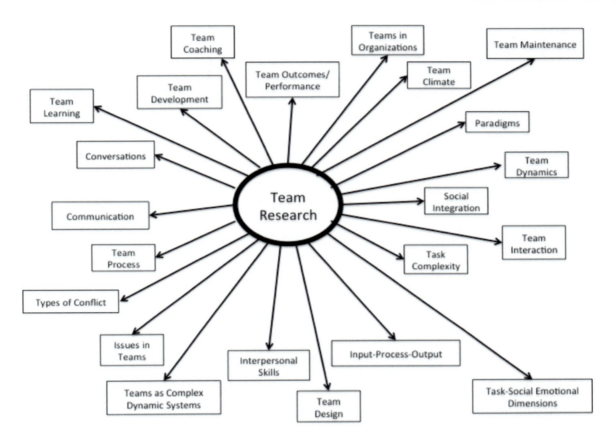

11.6 The Importance of Understanding Team Interaction

Today, being a member of an organization always involves being on a team. Whether you are a team member or a team leader, you will constantly engage in teams that go beyond just completing a job or task. Although numerous team theories or models exist in research and practice, very few look at team learning and development from the

> Recent research indicating the importance of team interaction aligns with our argument that central to the understanding of team experience in the work environment is the quality of each team's interaction.

perspective of a team's lived experience in comparison to what the members would like to experience. Yet most of the feedback or comments we get from team members are based on the discrepancy between what they hope to experience and what they actually experience as they engage with each other along task, nontask, leadership, and safety aspects. Recent research that focuses on team interaction aligns with our argument that central to the quality of team interaction is the quality of team experience. We will present understanding team interaction as an emergent area of research and practice.

Although research and theories that focus on the importance of interaction are becoming more prevalent, the experiences of interaction at the team level have not been examined in detail. As the experience of team interaction in organizations occurs at the work environment where they function, focusing on the work context of teams has become of particular interest to both researchers and practitioners.

In this book, we show how to capture interaction at the team level using the TLI, which focuses not only on the work context but also on the individual clients and supervisors who work with teams, creating a 360-degree team-level assessment that captures the actual and desired states of a team at any point in time and uses this to facilitate effective team-level coaching. This is particularly effective as it treats every team as unique, to be assessed and treated as such.

11.7 Mapping a Team's Quality of Engagement Using the Team Learning Inventory

In the previous chapter, we identified four major dimensions of team interaction that contribute to the quality of team engagement. Each dimension was defined, including its different aspects (for the diverging and converging dimensions). The diagram below maps the four major dimensions, showing both actual and desired interactions at that point in time.

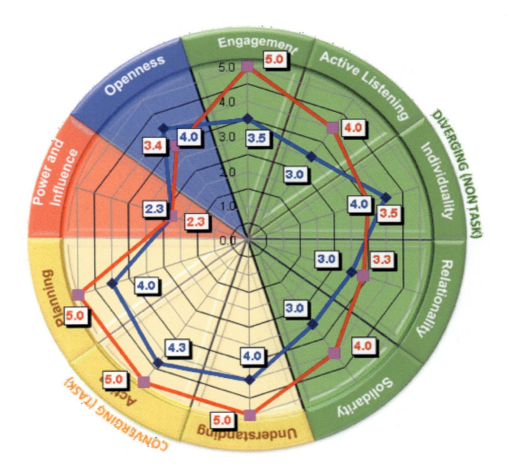

The above profile shows the actual state of a team's quality of engagement represented by a blue line and the desired state represented by a red line. Each of the colored sectors of the diagram represents one of the four major dimensions of team interaction, with the subsumed aspects for both the diverging and converging dimensions. The scores for both the actual and desired profiles are averaged from all team members.

We used established methods to identify the best model for creating a team-level score based on individual scores. During team coaching, the coach would work with the team as a whole to identify important aspects they would like to develop. Having both the actual and desired states would allow for effective team coaching.

To dive deeper into each of the dimensions scored by individual members, we provide a line diagram showing how each team member rated all ten aspects. This provides the team with information as to how each team member is experiencing the quality of engagement. Scores that are similar indicate similar experiences, and scores that are inconsistent suggest that team members differ in each of these aspects. The diagram below shows an example of a team's individual member ratings.

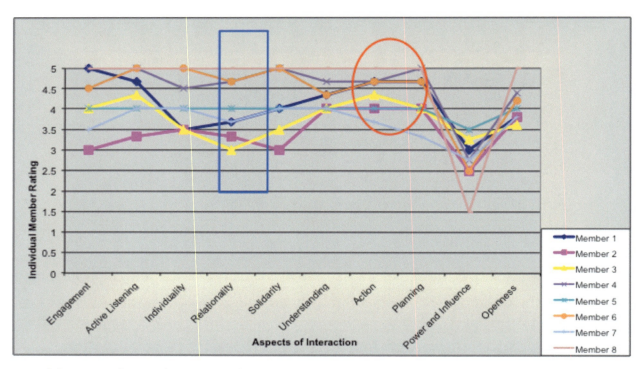

In addition to these charts, we also capture a team's assessment of how members rate their perception of how the team is performing, how satisfied they feel as team members, and how safe they feel when working in the team. As mentioned earlier, we also capture how clients and supervisors interact directly with the team. With this information, team members can understand how they are functioning within the larger system.

11.8 A Team's Innovation and Execution Capacities

As discussed in chapter 4, we also used various theories to develop both the innovation and execution capacities at the team level. We profile the team's actual and desired innovative and execution capacities. The diagram below shows an example of a team's innovative and execution capacities.

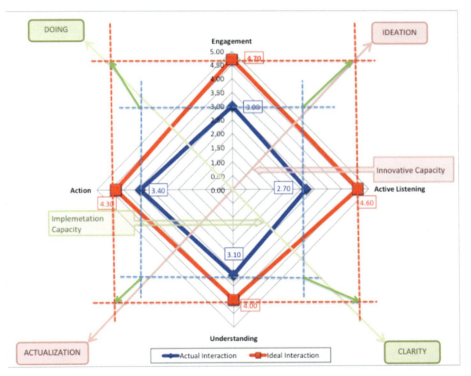

As can be seen in the above example, the blue and red lines and related dotted lines show the team's actual and desired capacities respectively. The lime green arrows represent the development that needs to occur to help the team reach desired capacities for innovation and execution.

The TLI methodology can be effectively applied to identify a team's quality of engagement and develop skills related to innovation and execution at the team level. This, together with individual team members' LNI results, would lead to high-impact engagement and promote better teamwork in organizations and educational institutions. This methodology, incorporating the use of a validated and robust measure (the TLI) with team coaching, can help leaders, managers, and educators improve performance at the individual and team levels. Developing individuals and teams using this method would ultimately help organizations adapt and thrive.

> The TLI can be an effective methodology to capture a team's quality of engagement and its innovative and execution capacities.

11.9 Using the TLI in Organizations and Educational Institutions

Over the years, we have used both the LNI and TLI in organizational and educational settings. As the TLI captures both quantitative and qualitative data from a team—that is, a team's actual and desired quality of engagement—with a reliable, valid, and robust tool before and after team coaching, we were able to show the results of evidence-based coaching. We have mentioned that despite billions of dollars spent on training and development programs, very few focus on teams and even fewer on teams within the work context. The TLI meets this requirement. Data collected using the TLI before team coaching (Time 1) and after coaching (Time 2) provides evidence of the effectiveness of the training and coaching of teams.

The concrete data collected using the TLI has recently been considered as an effective way to help develop interprofessional teams at the front line. Due to the fluid nature of membership at the front line (membership based on profession and not on individuals), it would be possible to collect data from each fluid team to establish an aggregate. This aggregated data and profile can be used to help frontline teams be more effective when directly involved with patients and their support network.

The TLI can also be used for the various types of teams in health care to identify different emphases based on four dimensions (e.g., in urgent care teams, the focus would be on developing the converging and the power and influence dimensions of teamwork, while departmental teams would be more holistic). Profiling the diverse types of teams in health care can promote effective team coaching for each of the types of teams by focusing on what works best for them.

The TLI can be effectively used in educational institutions to develop team-leadership and membership skills. A survey of corporate recruiters conducted by the Graduate Management Admissions Council states that 38 percent of recruiting organizations surveyed consider soft skills and teamwork skills extremely important when hiring MBA graduates. The trend for having students put into teams as part of program curricula has to be met with increased focus on developing team leadership and membership skills. Using the TLI as a way to evaluate student learning outcomes can be an effective demonstration of students developing team skills and support accreditation requirements with team-level data for assessing learning outcomes relating to teamwork.

Three practices mentioned in a 2008 report[44] identifying high-impact educational practices—learning communities, capstone projects, and service learning—can easily be assessed using the TLI when these involve teamwork. Action learning project teams, service learning teams, and some capstone projects would involve working with organizations in the community. The use of the TLI as a 360-degree assessment would naturally include clients and faculty

---

[44] G. D. Kuh, *High-Impact Educational Practices: What They Are, Who Has Access to Them, and Why They Matter* (Washington, DC: Association of American Colleges and Universities, 2008).

evaluations of the team. Further, the TLI would also allow team coaching as part of such courses to help students develop team-leadership and membership skills as well as client-management skills. We have used the TLI for action learning projects to help students develop these critical skills. Our finding that teams could improve after one month of team coaching shows the possible powerful impact with regards to developing team leadership and membership skills.

In the next chapter, we will discuss the evolution of team development since the 1950s; reveal how using the TLI aligns with recent theories of change that have emerged in the hard sciences; and provide evidence of team development in organizations and educational institutions.

Summary

1. The Team Learning Inventory (TLI) was developed based on experiential learning theory, conversational learning, team research, and creativity (design and innovation).

2. Team researchers can be fundamentally split into two groups: those who argue teamwork is very complex and it is best to zoom into specific aspects and those who argue that teamwork should be studied holistically.

3. Researchers, scholars, and practitioners have identified team interaction as critical to understanding the lived experience of teams at work.

4. The TLI is designed to capture a team's actual and desired quality of engagement and its innovation and execution capacities.

5. The TLI can be and has been used in organizations and educational institutions.

CHAPTER 12

Team Development and Evidence of Team Coaching Using the Team Learning Inventory

12.1 The Need for Team Training and Development

Across the globe, with the increasingly complex and volatile work environment, organizations are recognizing the importance of developing leaders and employees to increase internal capacity to innovate and enhance performance. A major shift in structural design to meet this need is to incorporate teams across all levels of organizations. Yet most training programs are focused on developing individuals' leadership and supervisory skills. As we have mentioned, very few team training and development programs offer team assessment and coaching within their work context.

The fundamental shift toward a team-oriented organizational environment has created a push to incorporate team skills training or team-development programs as an integral part of human resource development, especially since the constantly changing organizational environment requires team-level engagement to contribute to innovation and success in organizations. However, in both organizational and educational contexts, creating teams and having members deal with difficulties or frustrations on their own is not the answer. Today, many individual-focused leadership-training programs exist to help develop individuals, but programs to develop teams are still very much in an infantile stage.

> The fundamental shift to a team-oriented structure in organizations has created a push to incorporate team skills training or team-development programs as an integral part of human resources.

Despite the critical need for effective team development, the majority of team training is based on theories that have existed since the 1960s. Team-development theories have evolved dramatically since then. Tracking shifts in these theories, we uncovered that we could understand this evolution based on the scientific theories of change over time.

12.2 Theories of Team Development

Since change is inevitable but presents opportunities for improvement and growth, and team development has been established as valuable to organizations, in this chapter we discuss the evolution of team-development concepts, theories, and models, particularly in relation to change theories in the hard sciences during those periods. Here we will highlight ways in which the TLI's use for team training and development in the work context is aligned with more recent theories of nonlinear dynamic change.

> The evolution of theories and models of team development over time is intrinsically related to the change theories in the hard sciences in those time periods.

12.3 Team Development as Linear Change

Initially, team scholars presented linear models of teamwork, which subsequently shifted significantly to include more current complex and chaotic models. Such shifts in our understanding of teams is not surprising; they can be traced to scientific models of change available to team researchers over time. It is during the 1960s that team development began to be an area of focus, and this grew significantly in the 1970s and 1980s. Some of the major concepts and theories put forward include stage models, such as the familiar forming, storming, norming, and performing,[45] and phase models, such as orientation, interpersonal exploration, and production.[46] Most reviews done on team development put forward models that were largely linear in nature.[47] Although linear motion was presented by Newton in his three laws in 1687, the dominant scientific theory used in psychology studies and management in recent years were still based on this linear model of change. This approach was appealing to organizations, as it presented more predictable outcomes when quality control circles and work improvement teams became more common in the work environment.

12.4 Team Development as Linear Dynamic Change

General systems theory—including a feedback loop—was introduced in 1968 by von Bertalanffy, but this dynamic model did not become influential until the 1980s and 1990s.

---

[45] B. W. Tuckman, "Developmental Sequence in Small Groups," *Psychological Bulletin* 65, no. 6 (1965): 384–99.

[46] L. Gruner, "A Study of Group Development in Purposive Groups," (PhD dissertation, University of Southern California, 1972).

[47] For example: A. Chang, J. Duck, and P. Bordia, "Understanding the Multidimensionality of Group Development," *Small Group Research* 37, no. 4 (2006): 327–50; D. R. Ilgen, J. R. Hollenbeck, M. Johnson, and D. Jundt, "Teams in Organizations: From Input-Process-Output Models to IMOI Models," *Annual Review of Psychology* 56 (2005): 517–43; R. W. Woodman and J. J. Sherwood, "The Role of Team Development in Organizational Effectiveness: A Critical Review," *Psychological Bulletin* 88, no. 1 (1980): 166–86.

Adding a feedback loop transformed linear change to linear dynamic change. Team researchers began considering the inclusion of linear dynamics into team development. The input-process-output framework was seen as insufficient for characterizing teams, especially since teams are affected by external contexts and internal activities.[48] Stage models such as the one proposed by Tuckman's Forming-Storming-Norming-Performing model began to be reviewed and considered insufficient, as the development process in teams is more complex than can be reflected in a linear stage model,[49] which also does not reflect changes in groups over time.[50]

12.5 Introduction of Team Development as Nonlinear Dynamic Change

In the 1990s, the focus on the dynamic nature of teamwork and team interaction resulted in the emergence of nonlinear dynamics as an appropriate approach to studying the complex nature of teamwork and team development from the 1980s to the present. The inclusion of nonlinear dynamics into teamwork studies radically shifted our understanding of team development. As nonlinear dynamics is a broad category that includes complexity and chaos theories, we will peel this apart to show the evolution of our current understanding of team development.

Beginning with the introduction of nonlinear dynamics (not including complexity and chaos theories), team researchers realized that team development is actually more complex than

---

[48] K. L. Moreland, "Assessment of Validity in Computer-Based Interpretations," in *The Computer and the Decision-Making Process*, eds. T. B. Gutkin and S. L. Wise (Lawrence Erlbaum Associates, Inc., (1991), 43–74; S. W. J. Kozlowski and K. J. Klein, "A Multilevel Approach to Theory and Research in Organizations: Contextual, Temporal, and Emergent Processes," in *Multilevel Theory, Research, and Methods in Organizations: Foundations, Extensions, and New Directions*, eds. K. J. Klein and S. W. J. Kozlowski (San Francisco: Jossey-Bass, 2000), 3–90.

[49] E. Sundstrom, K. De Meuse, and D. Futrell, "Work Teams: Applications and Effectiveness," *American Psychologist* 45, no. 2 (1990): 120–33.

[50] T. Rickards and S. Moger, "Creative Leadership Processes in Project Team Development: An Alternative to Tuckman's Stage Model," *British Journal of Management* 11, no. 4 (2000): 273–83.

initially proposed.[51] The shift in perspective that teams are not linear but complex, adaptive, and dynamic systems required an understanding that teams develop from one state to another and that these states are emergent. Scholars aligned with this shift highlighted the importance of team interaction and its relation to the experience of teamwork.

12.6 Team Development Based on Complexity Theory, Chaos Theory, and the Principle of Computational Equivalence

Since the United States started using the Japanese concept of working with teams to create a better work environment in 1980s, the philosophy of continuous improvement has expanded, using complexity theory to include both continuous improvement (first-order change) and significant change (second-order change). Complexity theory[52] as a change model has not been given enough attention in terms of team development, particularly the process of incremental change (or first order) and radical change (or second order). Scholars who identify team interaction as part of team development agree that complexity theory is a better approach to understanding team development, as radical change is more powerful than incremental or linear change.

Scholars who focus on team interaction and/or team experience, in contrast, suggest a chaotic model of team development.[53] When considering team interaction as the central

---

[51] A. Fuhriman and G. M. Burlingame, "Measuring Small Group Process: A Methodological Application of Chaos Theory," *Small Group Research* 25 (1994): 502–18.

[52] B. Burnes, "Complexity Theories and Organizational Change," *International Journal of Management Reviews* 7, no. 2 (2005): 73–90.

[53] For example: A. P. Hare, "Roles, Relationships, and Groups in Organizations: Some Conclusions and Recommendations," *Small Group Research* 34, no. 2 (2003): 123–54; T. Lingham and B. Richley, "Teamwork: High-Impact Teams," in *The Sage Encyclopedia of Quality and the Service Economy*, ed. S. M. Dahlgaard-Park (Thousand Oaks, CA: Sage Publications, 2015); V. Wekselberg, W. C. Goggin, and T. J. Collings, "A Multifaceted Concept of Group Maturity and Its Measurement and Relationship to Group Performance, *Small Group Research* 28, no. 1 (1997): 3–28.

phenomenon that impacts team development, one could consider state 1 of the team as its interaction patterns at time 1 and state 2 as the developed state after an intervention to facilitate change and development. This aligns with the view that team interaction is idiosyncratic in nature and therefore unique to each team. It is perhaps clear to most scholars that teams are complex systems and therefore difficult to comprehend or measure well. As a result, most developmental models that are suggested as nonlinear, complex, or chaotic are theoretical and cannot capture team development over time.

One of the most recent theories that has emerged is the principle of computational equivalence (PCE)[54] introduced in 2002. PCE states that what appear to be highly complex and adaptive outcomes can be boiled down to simple fundamental patterns. As team interaction and team experience are both complex and adaptive from a holistic point of view, we should be able to identify simple patterns that cause such complexity to emerge.

12.7 Team Development Using the TLI

The Team Learning Inventory was designed and developed with the knowledge of recent nonlinear dynamic theories of change. When using the TLI to assess the quality of engagement and the innovation and execution capacities at that point in time, we are capturing state 1 of the team. As the profile for each team is unique to that team, that state is specifically for that team at that point in time. Based on chaos theory and PCE, the next state of the team (after coaching using the TLI) will be affected by the four fundamental dimensions (diverging; converging; power and influence; and

> The TLI is designed with knowledge of recent and current theories in the hard sciences. It captures initial and emergent states of any team, and the team-coaching methodology is focused on helping teams develop toward their desired state at that point in time.

---

[54] Wolfram, *A New Kind of Science* (Champaign, IL: Wolfram Media, 2002).

openness) addressed collaboratively by the team and the coach. The team coaching session is based on all data collected from state 1.

As mentioned earlier, the data would include the four dimensions, depicting the following:

- actual and desired quality of engagement
- variance of team members' ratings
- team members' outcome assessments
- team's actual and desired innovative and execution capacities
- qualitative comments from team members
- quantitative and qualitative evaluations from external evaluators

Using the actual state and the desired state at that point in time, the coach would engage with the team to identify and work on specific behaviors that would move the team toward its ideal state at that point in time.

After the coaching session, and allowing four to six months for the team to practice new behaviors, the TLI is administered again to capture the new emergent state of the team (or state 2). Again, this emergent state is unique to that team. As the TLI captures both qualitative and quantitative data, assessment at state 2 can be compared to state 1 to show the team's development. This state 2 is the new state 1 of the team.

12.8 Evidence-Based Team Training and Development

Prior research demonstrates that a good training program is one that is developed around experiential learning theory[55] such that participants can learn and apply what they've learned. Our own research

> Team training and development programs in organizations should be designed to provide organizations with evidence of team development.

---

[55] R. Vince, "Behind and beyond Kolb's Learning Cycle," *Journal of Management Education* 22, no. 3 (1998): 304–19.

extended this to identify three aspects of training and development critical to successful programs: content, applicability, and perceived importance of the session.[56]

With the expectation that team training programs should result in team learning and development, attention must turn to one of the most important aspects in training: evidence of development. Although numerous individual-level training programs exist, there are hardly equivalent programs that focus on team assessment, coaching, and development.

12.9 Evidence of Team Development in Organizations Using the TLI

Over the years, we have done numerous sessions of team training and team coaching using the TLI. As an example, we did a training program for fifty-four teams in a Midwest organization over four years. Teams attended the training program, and we assessed each team's quality of engagement. They then underwent our team-coaching process, and we assessed quality of engagement four to five months later. We wanted to show that teams going through our program of assessment and coaching at the team level do improve their experience in the work environment. We also wanted to see if the development from precoaching (time 1) to postcoaching (time 2) was significantly better.

Using paired t-test analysis, our results were very encouraging. We could show that the teams did develop in terms of the gap between their actual and desired quality of engagement at work. Without going into hypothesis testing and statistical support, across all fifty-four teams, the gap between actual and desired engagement was smaller in time 2 compared to time 1. We also showed that the gap between the desired and actual experience in time 2 was smaller than the gap in time 1. This indicates that after the team coaching session, there was a

---

[56] T. Lingham, B. A. Richley, and D. Rezania, "An Evaluation System for Training Programs: A Case Study Using a Four-Phase Approach," *Career Development International Journal* 11, no. 4 (2006): 334–51.

much smaller gap at the significant level of .068 in the teams' assessment, demonstrating with empirical evidence that the teams do develop.

We also had evidence to show that the reduction in the gap between the desired experience and the actual experience from time 1 to time 2 does impact the internal evaluation from the team members. Using regression analysis, we show that with a unit decrease in the gap from times 1 to 2, a team's internal evaluation reduces by .31 units (at the significant level of .05). The finding is indeed clear evidence that after the team-coaching process, teams did actually develop.

The external evaluators rated the team significantly higher (or better) in time 2 versus time 1 (significant level of .059). This is another demonstration of the development of the team with evidence to support that the team, as part of a larger system, did better after team coaching.

12.10 Evidence of Team Development in Educational Settings Using the TLI

12.10.1. Management: Action Learning

As discussed earlier, the Graduate Management Admissions Council supported the need for teamwork skills more than a decade ago in its 2006 Corporate Recruiters Survey Report. This in turn has resulted in an aligned shift in academia as educators and leaders recognize the dire need to include teamwork in their programs to produce graduates who have team skills. An example of such an effort is action learning.

Based on feedback from clients, recruiters, coaches, faculty, and students, we updated the action learning program to drive individual and team development, with the primary focus on experiential learning. The three major components were as follows:

1. Having students work on a real-life corporate project
2. Having students work in teams while providing the opportunity for students to develop team leadership and membership skills through the use of an assessment to capture team interaction and allow participants to rate the performance of their team, how satisfied they are as members, and also how safe they feel in the team as they go through their work on these projects
3. Incorporating team coaching as part of the program

Although most action learning programs offer real-life projects in such designs, the second component may not be equally weighted. In order to incorporate the second component into an action learning program, we included the TLI and team coaching for these teams.

The new twelve-week design incorporates an initial assessment of the team in week 3 followed by team coaching and a six-week experiment with new behaviors to improve team interaction. In week 9, we repeated the TLI. A total of nine teams of three to five members participated.

The diagram below shows the mappings of one team. Our results show that the self-report team results (performance, member satisfaction, and psychological safety) all had increases ranging from 4.2 percent to almost 10 percent. The mappings show not only improvement in real interaction but also a reduction in the gaps between real and ideal interaction. The labels used in the diagram below were earlier labels, with the updated labels discussed in chapter 12.

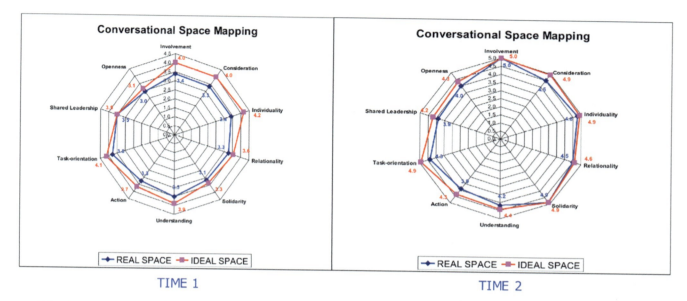

TIME 1   TIME 2

The improved real interaction in time 2 was a result of effective team coaching to help the team practice new behaviors to reduce gaps that the team considered most critical to their effectiveness as a team. At the end of the program, the qualitative feedback from students in the course evaluations highlighted the usefulness of the team-coaching segment of the action learning program.

12.10.2. Health Care: Nursing Management Course

In a nursing management course focusing on teamwork skills (specifically on relationship and task skills), the TLI was used to capture relationship skills using the diverging dimension and the task skills using the converging dimension. A sample of ninety-four prelicensure nursing students was divided into twenty teams. Students were asked to self-select into teams during the initial class meeting. The purpose of the course was to complete six team assignments. The assignments measured the students' knowledge of management skills using six nursing-management case studies in presentation formats. After three team assignments, students completed the TLI. Then, the even-numbered groups were coached, using a structured process, and odd-numbered groups were not. Following the completion of three more case study assignments and presentations, the TLI was repeated.

The means of both the diverging and converging dimensions in the "not coached" and "coached" teams increased from preintervention. Using a repeated measure, ANOVA, the means of the diverging dimension between not coached and coached groups from preintervention to postintervention was significant at .003; the converging dimension between the not-coached and coached teams was significant at .065.

The results indicate that the coaching intervention had an effect on both the diverging and converging dimensions. The coaching intervention provided an opportunity for coached teams of students to discuss teamwork relationship issues, such as listening carefully to each other, sharing unique viewpoints, and considering all sides of an issue before acting on it. Coached by faculty, students were able to identify short-term goals and plan how to practice relationship skills while completing their tasks for the class assignments. This supports the hypothesis that a structured team-coaching process can contribute to student team-skill development.

Summary

1. The fundamental shift to a team-oriented structure in organizations has created a push to incorporate team-skills training or team-development programs as an integral part of human resources.

2. The evolution of theories and models of team development over time are intrinsically related to change theories in the hard sciences in the same periods.

3. The Team Learning Inventory is designed with recent and current theories in the hard sciences. The TLI captures initial and emergent states of any team, and the team-coaching methodology is focused on helping teams develop toward their desired state at that point in time.

4. Team training and development programs in organizations should be designed to provide them with evidence of team development.

Reflecting on Your Team Training and Development Experience

Answer the following questions from your own experience being involved in team training and development programs in your current or previous organizations:

1. What theory or theories of change were used to guide the team training programs? Identify as many as you can.

On this side of the page, write down the theory or theories of change used for team development.	On this side of the page, write down which theories of change in the hard sciences apply.

2. What did you learn about teams or teamwork from these training programs?

On this side of the page, write what you learned about teams or teamwork.	On this side of the page, write down what you would have liked to learn.

Putting It All Together: Our Approach to High-Impact Engagement

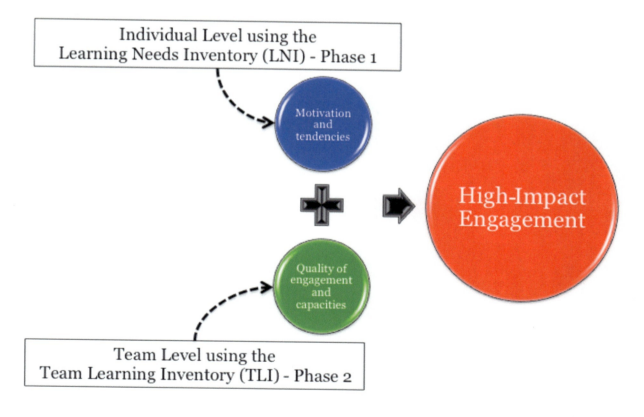

Individual Level using the
Learning Needs Inventory (LNI) - Phase 1

Motivation and tendencies

Quality of engagement and capacities

High-Impact Engagement

Team Level using the
Team Learning Inventory (TLI) - Phase 2

CHAPTER 13

Developing High-Impact Engagement: Putting It All Together

13.1 High-Impact Engagement

As we discussed in chapter 2, high-impact engagement is a melding of both individual and team levels in our work. We develop high-impact engagement in two phases: one at the individual and interpersonal level and the other at the team level. At the individual and interpersonal level, we focus on individuals' underlying motivational needs and their innovation and execution tendencies. At the team level, we use the Team Learning Inventory (TLI) to focus on team-level quality of engagement and the team's innovation and execution capacities. We will first revisit phase 1.

13.2 Phase 1: Individual- and Interpersonal-Level Assessment and Development

When working with others, it is important to be aware of one's own motivational needs. As discussed in phase 1 (chapters 3 through 7), the Learning Needs Inventory (LNI) was designed to capture an individual's adaptability profile as well as innovation and execution tendencies. Further, the LNI was developed using established theories—experiential learning theory (ELT), learning flexibility, creativity (design and innovation), motivation theories, and in particular work motivation. These theories highlight dynamics in the work environment that are extremely useful and even valuable for meaningful individual learning and development.

13.3 Phase 1: Developing the First and Second Aspects of Adaptability

Insights from the LNI not only promote individual-level awareness but simultaneously develop higher levels of interpersonal awareness. This awareness is focused on having the skill to listen for framing instead of content, which can be taught and developed using the LNI in a team setting. The experience of working with others improves tremendously when team members realize that most interactions, reactions, support, and engagement are largely the manifestation of the underlying motivational needs of individuals. Developing the flexibility to either listen and engage or align with such needs would create an entirely different approach to interacting with others. This skill will also be linked to an ability to adapt to changing situations and manage upward with equal success.

In addition to helping team members become more skilled at the first aspect of adaptability, the LNI is designed to help them develop more balanced tendencies when engaging in innovation and execution. The LNI can further be used for developing innovation and execution tendencies relevant to work, identity, or function in their profession. When individuals complete the LNI (which takes two to three minutes), they receive a report that includes the following:

- definitions of the underlying learning needs and a personal score for each
- overall adaptability profile
- details of innovation and execution tendencies
- overall innovation and execution tendencies profile
- workbook for creating a learning and development plan
- facilitator guidebook for coaches (provided for certified LNI coaches; individuals interested in being certified should contact admin@interaction-science.com)

13.4 Phase 1: Purpose of the LNI

The LNI helps individuals realize the following:

- how and why they frame statements the way they do
- how adaptable they are at work
- their innovation and execution tendencies

The LNI is behavior based and specifically designed for coaching and development focused on adaptability, innovation, and execution skills. As the LNI is based on behavioral tendencies, it will do the following:

- raise individual-level awareness
- raise awareness of others
- increase others' feelings of being heard and appreciated
- increase levels of engagement

This is especially useful for team-leadership coaching and development by Interaction Science, LLC, certified coaches.

We now revisit phase 2 of the methodology.

13.5 Phase 2: Team-Level Assessment and Development

When working with others, particularly in teams, it is critical to understand the fundamental dimensions of team interaction. We discussed phase 2 of our methodology from chapters 8 through 12, including the fact that teams are ubiquitous in organizational and educational contexts; the importance of team training and development (particularly in the work context); the continuum of team experience; and the emergence of the centrality of team interaction to understand team experience. We then looked into how teams have been studied since the 1950s as well as theories of team development that existed from that period until today. We presented the nature of team interaction based on research and practice we have done over the past fifteen years.

Finally, we presented the design of the TLI, created by incorporating existing theories (experiential learning theory, conversational learning, team research, team development, and creativity, innovation, and design concepts). We also explained that the TLI is designed to capture a team's actual and desired quality of engagement as well as innovation and execution capacities. We further pointed out that the approach to team development using the TLI aligns with current theories of change in the hard sciences (particularly chaos theory and the principle of computational equivalence).

We believe that the TLI is very effective in team training and development, especially focusing on team members' experience in the work context, and also provides evidence-based team coaching. Apart from team coaching, in team training programs we have conducted, the TLI has also helped team leaders realize that team leadership is somewhat different from leadership. A team leader has to be conscious of the quality of engagement; shifts of learning needs as team members engage; how to leverage innovation and execution capacities and/or develop them; and attending to the four major dimensions of team interaction. One of the most significant shifts is the team leader's ability to create a team that can actively contribute, and influence the larger system and not be dependent on her/him or any one particular member.

13.6 Phase 2: Developing a Team's Quality of Engagement

Using the TLI, we are able to capture the quality of engagement of any team at a particular point in time, which we present as state 1 of the team. In this assessment, we capture both the actual and desired quality of engagement of the team. As the assessment has been tested as reliable, valid, and robust (since we tested and used it in teams across industries, cultures, and countries), the four fundamental dimensions of team interaction (diverging; converging; power and influence; and openness) have been shown to be present in all types of teams in diverse organizations and educational institutions. Using the principle of computational equivalence and chaos theory, the four dimensions are the fundamental pattern of team interaction and captured as state 1 of the team.

Based on the profiles of the actual and desired quality of team engagement (and the gaps across all ten aspects in the four dimensions), team coaches certified by Interaction Science, LLC, will be able to coach the team to develop toward its ideal state. After a few months to allow members to practice new behaviors, we can assess state 2 of the team, with both states unique to the team. Such an assessment, coaching, and development methodology is aligned with current theories of change relevant to the work context, with the ability to show evidence-based team development.

13.7 Phase 2: Developing a Team's Innovation and Execution Capacities

Using the TLI for teams, we are able to capture the actual and desired innovation and execution capacities of the team in state 1. Based on the profile and resulting capacities of innovation and execution (both actual and desired), the team coach is able to help teams move their capacities toward their desired profile. Again, after a few months of allowing team members to practice new norms and behaviors, we are able to capture teams' actual and desired innovation and execution capacities in state 2.

The TLI is valuable for teams that have worked together for at least a month and for team leaders taking over leadership of a team that they have worked with or are leading for the first time. During a global organization team training and development program, one country manager who had just taken over leadership of the country team that underwent team training and development mentioned to us that he learned what would help his team during the training session using the TLI, without which it would have taken him a year to figure out. We have used the TLI in a team-development retreat for a top management team to identify the innovation and execution tendencies of each member and how those align with the intent of the team to develop a balanced capacity for the two aspects of innovation and execution. Such approaches with diverse intent of team training and development are very possible, as the TLI captures the team experience in the work context.

Team members take about twenty to twenty-five minutes to complete the TLI. The report includes the following:

- response rates
- details of each dimension and the team's scores
- overall mapping of the quality of engagement
- variance of team members' ratings
- assessment of team performance, member satisfaction, and psychological safety
- qualitative comments from team members
- evaluation of the team from bosses and clients who work with the team directly
- details of the team's innovation and execution capacities
- overall profile of the team's innovation and execution capacities

- workbook for the team
- facilitator guidebook for coaches (provided for certified TLI coaches; individuals interested in being certified should contact admin@interaction-science.com)

13.8 Phase 2: Purpose of the TLI

The TLI profiles a team's current and desired states of engagement (interaction) based on the lived experience of a team within the work environment. As the TLI is both experience and behavior based, it captures a team's current innovation and execution capacities. A team coach is able to help the team achieve its desired state of engagement and desired innovation and execution capacities. This process helps a team contribute and influence larger systems, resulting in high-impact engagement.

13.9 Combining Phase 1 and Phase 2: Developing High-Impact Engagement

Combining the LNI and TLI, team members receive information at the individual and team levels. The diagram below shows what each team member would receive.

LNI Report	TLI Report
1. Definitions of the Underlying Learning Needs and your score for each of them	1. Response rates
	2. Details of each dimension and the team's scores
2. Your overall adaptability profile	3. Overall mapping of the quality of engagement
3. Details of innovation and execution tendencies	4. Variance of team members' ratings
	5. Assessment of team performance, member satisfaction, and psychological safety
4. Your overall innovation and execution tendencies profile	6. Qualitative comments from team members
5. A workbook for the creating a learning and development plan	7. Evaluation of the team from bosses and clients that work with the team directly
6. A Facilitator Guidebook for coaches	8. Details of the team's innovation and execution capacities
	9. An overall profile of the team's innovation and execution capacities
	10. A workbook for the team
	11. A Facilitator Guidebook for coaches

13.10 Combining Phase 1 and Phase 2: The Process

When engaging with organizations to conduct training and development for teams or if asked to work with a particular team, it would be important to know what the intent is at the team level or higher. With that information in mind, as consultants or trainers, we usually present the information the team would need to know (i.e., foundational works and theories at the individual and team levels) without empirical support from research. Team members would then complete the TLI over two weeks—especially if they request the 360-degree version of it. During that time frame, the members should complete the LNI on-site (which is feasible, as it is online and takes approximately two minutes).

We then schedule individual coaching sessions with each member separately as part of that individual's learning and development process. Once the coaching is completed, the team meets again, and members present themselves based on their individual LNI profiles and underlying motivational needs. Allow for interaction to take place as members get to know each other better or achieve insight and awareness of how other members have been framing issues, concerns, and suggestions.

Members will also present their innovation and execution tendencies and how they would like to develop these skills further. The team leader can point out how projects or tasks have been framed so as to understand what is needed and how to ensure success of projects or tasks moving forward. At this point, members will also get to understand underlying motivational needs or shifts at the higher or organizational level.

Upon presentation of the TLI report, a separate training session is provided to help the team make sense of the results. Afterward, the coach or trainer will schedule a two-hour team-coaching session to help members develop new behaviors and norms as they move toward their desired state. After four to six months of practicing these new behaviors and norms, the team completes the TLI again to capture development and evolution. Another session is provided for the team to review the TLI results at time 1 (state 1) and time 2 (state 2).

The following is a succinct presentation of the steps in each of the phases:

- Phase 1: individual-level training, development, and coaching
    - Phase 1a: ELT and LSI (half day)
    - Phase 1b: LNI (half day)
    - Phase 1c: individual coaching with LNI (one hour per team member/individual one-on-one)

- Phase 2: team-level training, development, and coaching
  - Phase 2a: completing the TLI (two weeks to complete internal and external)
  - Phase 2b: training session for TLI (half day)
  - Phase 2c: team coaching session (half hour with team leader; two hours with team; half hour with team leader)
  - Phase 2d: practicing new behaviors (minimum time: two months)
  - Phase 2e: completing the TLI (time 2; two weeks to complete internal and external)
  - Phase 2f: training workshop with TLI times 1 and 2; half day)

By combining the LNI and TLI, individuals and teams will develop awareness and skills to achieve high-impact engagement. Individuals will understand how to identify and attend to their own and others' underlying learning needs when working on tasks or projects. They will be able to contribute effectively to team-level capacities. Teams will be able to actively contribute and influence higher systems in which they are embedded and ultimately the organization itself.

ABOUT THE AUTHORS

Tony Lingham, PhD, and Bonnie Richley, PhD, are cofounders of Interaction Science, LLC, a management consulting company. Interaction Science offers individual and team coaching certification using the Learning Needs Inventory (LNI) and the Team Learning Inventory (TLI), as well as train-the-trainer certification.

Both authors are educated in interdisciplinary fields ranging from English literature, engineering, music, and psychology to organization development and organizational behavior. They have been organization, team, and leadership consultants for more than fifteen years, working with managers and leaders in national and multinational companies across the United States, Europe, Africa, and Asia, in both the for-profit and nonprofit sectors.

Prior to entering academia, they held leadership roles in organizations and as consultants. As academics and researchers, they have taught at the undergraduate, graduate, and doctoral levels in management schools and executive education in the United States, Europe, and Asia. Both have been nominated and awarded for teaching excellence on numerous occasions. As researchers, they have published multiple papers in academic and practitioner journals, presented at national and international conferences, and been keynote speakers at various professional organizations.

Both authors codeveloped the learning needs theory of motivation and the LNI at the individual level, and the focus on interaction and TLI at the team level. They are spearheading the global effort to create a structured process for evidence-based team coaching involving the assessment of actual and desired states of team interaction and how these profiles relate to the innovative and execution capacities of a team. Their work on the LNI and TLI has been tested and validated for more than fifteen years, with teams ranging from boards to functional teams and across countries (United States, Latin America, China, and Europe). They have presented a webinar on advanced team coaching and a webcast on high-impact engagement. They have been keynote speakers and panelists on various topics for numerous events and conferences in many countries for business and healthcare sectors.

Dr. Richley is coauthor of the book *Managing by Values: A Corporate Guide to Living, Being Alive, and Making a Living in the 21st Century*. Dr. Lingham has coauthored a textbook, *The Fundamentals of International Organiztional Behavior*. Both are certified senior executive and master coaches on emotional intelligence. At the personal level, the authors are a happy family with their puppy, Rosie. They enjoy watching documentaries, playing games on their iPhones, and having wonderful conversations over coffee in the morning while snuggling with Rosie.

APPENDIX A

Development of the Learning Needs Inventory (LNI)—Design and Analysis

A.1 Item Development

Based on our learning needs theory of motivation, we developed a scale to measure learning needs for each style. The initial pool of twenty-eight items (seven items per learning style) was developed over eighteen months and sent to experts for review for face validity. As we have also worked extensively with experiential learning theory and learning styles, our expertise and experience were also used to check the development of each item in the pool. We used a five-point scale to measure each item.[57] Items were only included after extensive discussion

---

[57] R. A. Peterson, "A Meta-Analysis of Cronbach's Coefficient Alpha," *Journal of Consumer Research* 21 (1994): 381–91.

and review and finally tested in a pilot study.[58] After removing influential and problematic items, the items remaining were reviewed in-depth by the authors and refined.

A final set of twenty-four items (six items per style) was selected for further testing, with the intent of keeping an equal number of items per style. This set of items was used over two years to collect enough respondents (our intent was to collect up to five responses per item). We managed to collect a total of 207 responses for our initial sample to test the twenty-four-item measure. Data screening and cleaning ended up with 205 responses that were used for our initial analysis. We tested the four-factor model and had to refine the items and reword them to capture face validity more accurately. We then tested the refined inventory by collecting more data for exploratory factor analysis (EFA) and confirmatory factor analysis (CFA).

A.2 Findings from Our Initial Analysis (EFA)

After collecting enough data (n=636), we cleaned the overall sample and ended up with a total of 615 responses, which we used for both EFA and CFA. For our EFA, we took 30 percent of the sample (n=186), and the data was analyzed using using principal axis factoring and promax rotation.[59] Results show a four-factor solution but with some items having problematic cross-loadings or loading on other factors. We systematically analyzed each factor and ended up

---

[58] P. E. Spector, "Summated Rating Scale Construction," *Sage University Paper Series on Quantitative Applications in the Social Sciences*, 07-082 (Thousand Oaks, CA: Sage Publications, 1992); R. G. Netemeyer, W. O. Bearden, and S. Sharma, *Scaling Procedures: Issues and Applications* (Thousand Oaks, CA: Sage Publications, 2003); R. F. DeVellis, *Scale Development: Theory and Applications* (Thousand Oaks, CA: Sage Publications, 2003).

[59] H. H. Harman, *Modern Factor Analysis*, 3rd ed. (Chicago: University of Chicago Press, 1976); J. Kim and C. W. Mueller, "Introduction to Factor Analysis: What It Is and How to Do It," *Sage University Paper Series in Quantitative Applications in the Social Sciences*, 07-013 (Thousand Oaks, CA: Sage Publications, 1978); E. J. Pedhazur and L. P. Schmelkin, *Measurement, Design, and Analysis: An Integrated Approach* (Hillsdale, NJ: Lawrence Erlbaum Associates, 1991).

with a set of sixteen items that were robust and loading as we had conceptualized, according to the underlying need in each style. The sample demographics are shown in the table below.

Table 1.
Demographics of Sample (n=615)

Type of Group	
Educational[a]	462
Work[b]	153
Gender	
Female	328
Male	287
Age Group	
60 years or older	8
50-59 years old	37
40-49 years old	97
30-39 years old	148
20-29 years old	321
19 years and younger	4

More details of the sample are indicated as follows:

- Educational groups ranged from graduate to doctoral levels.
- Graduate students were from master's programs in organizational development; operations and supply chain; full-time MBA, part-time, global MBA (China, India, and US), and nonprofit programs.
- Doctoral students were from executive doctoral programs and organizational behavior PhD programs.
- Work groups included IT professionals (US), university staff from various departments (US), professionals from an international hotel chain (China), professionals from a manufacturing/chemical organization (US), and senior professionals from Latin America.

Table 2 below shows the EFA loadings and correlations from the sample of 186 respondents (30 percent of the full data collected). We also include an example of an item developed for each underlying learning need in table 2. As can be seen in the table below, there were only two items that linked (or loaded) with other factors (i.e., item 20 and item 5). Based on established criteria of rigor for EFA, loadings less than 0.3 are acceptable. Although item 5 has a seemingly cross-loading of greater than 0.3, the negative loading implies that there is not a problem with the cross-loading.

Furthermore, the factors are not strongly correlated with each other based on the established criteria of rigor (i.e., correlations greater than 0.6 are problematic). As the range of the correlations is -0.085 to 0.456, the factors are indeed distinctly different from each other. Hence our findings from the EFA are encouraging and meet the standards of rigor established in this analysis, which then allowed us to proceed with the CFA for the remaining 70 percent of the data.

In the CFA analysis, we are essentially testing if this four-factor measurement model with the items as indicated within each factor would have a good fit with the remaining 70 percent of the data. Researchers report this using fit indices with established standards of rigor to confirm the initial measurement model from the EFA analysis.

Table 2.
Pattern Matrix from EFA[a] (30%, n=186) of Full Dataset arranged by Factors

Items[b]	Factors			
	1	2	3	4
Item 1	0.752			
Item 3	0.832			
Item 11	0.673			
Item 16	0.551			
Item 2		0.606		
Item 10		0.815		
Item 18		0.545		
Item 21		0.586	0.263	
Item 4			0.699	
Item 9			0.58	
Item 12			0.455	
Item 20	-0.204		0.655	0.252
Item 5			-0.278	0.388[c]
Item 6				0.622
Item 19				0.572
Item 24				0.679
Factor Correlation Matrix				
Factor	1	2	3	4
1	1			
2	0.063	1		
3	-0.085	0.277	1	
4	0.456	0.305	0.233	1
Examples of Items for Each Factor				
Factor	Sample Items			
1	I prefer to establish clear goals before work gets done			
2	I prefer discussing to explore or build ideas			
3	I prefer working fast on tasks/projects			
4	I prefer when criteria or expectations are developed to ensure tasks/projects are manageable			

Details of the analysis are as follows:

- EFA was conducted using principal axis factoring extraction and promax rotation.
- We maintained a model that would have equal numbers of items per factor.
- We kept item 5 because we wanted four items per factor and also because the cross-loading on factor 3 was negative.

A.3 Findings from Our CFA to Test Our Initial Measurement Model

Having refined the items from our EFA, we then tested the measurement model through CFA using Analysis of Moment Structures (AMOS) software. We used the remaining 70 percent of the data (n=430) and ran the CFA using the EFA as the model. Our model fit indices indicate that the model is acceptable based on established criteria. Table 3 shows the CFA results.

Table 3.
CFA Results with 70% of the data (n=430)

χ^2	CMIN	DF	P CMIN/DF
Initial Model	218.6	97	2.25
Model 1	141.5	92	1.54

Model Fit	NFI	RFI	IFI	TLI	CFI	RMSEA	PCLOSE
Initial Model	0.859	0.826	0.916	0.895	0.915	0.054	0.233
Model 1	0.909	0.881	0.966	0.955	0.965	0.035	0.986

The above table reports all the necessary fit indices (NFI, RFI, IFI, TLI, CFI, RSMEA, and PCLOSE) to meet the standards of rigor for CFA analysis as established in measurement theory. These are as follows:

- All parameter estimates were significant at $p<.000$.

- In model 1, we only correlated error terms with modification indices >10. All fit index criteria are acceptable.
- The overall reliability of the scale (Cronbach α) is 0.730.

The measurement model supports the learning needs theory of motivation as we theorized. The LNI can be used to measure the extent to which individuals need different learning motivational needs based on the learning needs theory of motivation. We are able to show that the higher the need in each of these dimensions, the higher the inherent need of the individual. We propose that in alignment with learning needs, situational needs also involve information, developing clarity, working with parameters, and finally getting things done. Aligning with situational needs is another level of flexibility. As this is both a diagnostic and prescriptive tool, the LNI can also be used as part of individual coaching to raise individual and interpersonal awareness.

Our measurement model's robustness and reliability permits us to use the LNI as both a diagnostic and prescriptive tool. As a mapping system, the LNI can be used to profile individuals' inherent learning needs, which may align (or not) to situational needs when working in a team. Hence, we believe that the LNI can be a very useful tool to help individuals develop learning flexibility (i.e., to align with different phases of project work from a learning perspective) and to develop their own capacity to innovate or execute in the work environment.

APPENDIX B

Development of the Team Learning Inventory (TLI)—Design and Analyses

B.1 Item Development

In identifying a good theory focused on the experiential nature of team interaction, we identified the theory of conversational learning[60] that is developed based on qualitative empirical data. In this theory, conversational learning is comprised of five pairs of dialectics:

1. Apprehension (APP) ↔ Comprehension (COM)
2. Intension (INT) ↔ Extension (EXT)
3. Individuality (IND) ↔ Relationality (REL)
4. Status (STA) ↔ Solidarity (SOL)
5. Discursive (DIS) ↔ Recursive (REC)

---

[60] A. C. Baker, P. J. Jensen, and D. A. Kolb, eds., *Conversational Learning: An Experiential Approach to Knowledge Creation* (Westport, CT: Quorum Books, 2002).

Based on this theory, we came up with five items that were then developed for each dialectical pole, creating a total of fifty items. The instrument was sent to experts on conversational learning and colleagues for an initial assessment of face validity.[61]

B.2 Findings from Our Initial Analysis (Exploratory Factor Analysis)

We tested our initial pool of items in a pilot study[62] on a representative sample of the intended population. After removing influential and problematic items, TLI items were analyzed from the 118 respondents from four classes of MBA students from a Midwestern university who had worked in their teams for more than a month. Based on the correlation and reliability studies, the items were further refined over four months to obtain better face and content validity. The final set of the revised fifty questions was administered to the research sample (n=377, 185 males and 192 females). In the research sample, we had MBA, non-MBA, and work groups. A total of 344 (91.3 percent of 377) cases were kept after removing missing cases and outliers. Forty-eight groups were represented, with group sizes ranging from five to twenty-six. The sample had an average of 7.54 members (3.7 males and 3.84 females). This sample was used to create the TLI and test it for dimensionality and to validate team interaction as a group-level construct.

Due to the sample size, and in order to maintain high standards of rigor, 120 permutated exploratory factor analyses using principal axis factoring and promax rotation were conducted on the entire data set for all ten poles of the real interactions. Thirty-five items were robust and embedded in four factors. We also ran four other sets of EFA permutations for the four sets of groups (educational, work, MBA, and non-MBA) to see if the results were robust. Thirty-five

---

[61] R. F. DeVellis, *Scale Development: Theory and Applications* (Thousand Oaks, CA: Sage Publications, Inc., 2003).

[62] R. G. Netemeyer, W. O. Bearden, and S. Sharma, *Scaling Procedures: Issues and Applications* (Thousand Oaks, CA: Sage Publications, 2003).

items were robust across the groups. The final four-factor (thirty-five item) model was used. The factors, their loadings, and correlations are shown in table 1.

As our intent was to develop a measure that captures a phenomenon at the team level while getting responses from team members, it would need to have characteristics of composition models where a construct operationalized at one level of analysis is related to another form of that construct at a different level of analysis. Based on compositional modeling,[63] the most appropriate model for this study was the direct consensus model, as the within-group agreement represents the shared perceptual agreement at the team level.

---

[63] D. Chan, "Functional Relations among Constructs in the Same Content Domain at Different Levels of Analysis: A Typology of Composition Models" *Journal of Applied Psychology* 83, no. 2 (1998): 234–46.

Table 1.
Exploratory Factor Analysis, Reliabilities, Intraclass Correlations and r_{wg} for
Individual Items and Factors (n= 341)

ITEMS	Exploratory Factor Analysis Factors and Loadings				F	ICC for Items	Factors	Cronbach's α for Factors	ICC for Factors[a] $(r_{wg}{}^{c})$
	1	2	3	4					
APP3	0.76				2.62	0.2***			
APP4	0.92		-0.21		5.05	0.4***			
APP5[d]	0.43		0.28		2.37	0.2***			
INT1	0.70				4.92	0.4***			
INT3	0.67				2.68	0.2***			
INT5	0.87		-0.21		4.36	0.4***			
IND1[d]	0.74				4.98	0.4***			
IND3	0.71				5.12	0.4***	Diverging	0.94	0.4*** (0.96)
IND5	0.57				3.64	0.3***			
REL1	0.73				3.67	0.3***			
REL4	0.77				4.42	0.4***			
REL5	0.75				1.92	0.2**			
SOL1	0.54			-0.25	3.27	0.3***			
SOL2[d]	0.42		0.22	-0.20	3.59	0.3***			
SOL4	0.77				3.95	0.3***			
SOL5[d]	0.48	0.31		-0.23	4.42	0.4***			
COM1	0.20	0.59			2.23	0.2***			
COM2		0.66			2.52	0.2***			
COM3[d]		0.48			2.55	0.2***			
COM5	0.21	0.49			1.71	0.1**			
EXT2		0.87			3.88	0.3**	Converging	0.90	0.2*** (0.95)
EXT4		0.60			3.17	0.3***			
EXT5		0.69			3.69	0.3***			
DIS1		0.73			3.53	0.3***			
DIS2		0.83			3.46	0.3***			
DIS4		0.83			2.95	0.3***			
STA1				0.63	2.49	0.2***			
STA2				0.75	4.07	0.4***	Power & Influence	0.75	0.4*** (0.76)
STA3				0.64	1.91	0.2**			
STA5				0.63	5.16	0.4***			
REC1			0.60		1.56	0.1*			
REC2			0.76		1.98	0.2***			
REC3			0.71		2.43	0.2***	Openness	0.82	0.3*** (0.90)
REC4			0.67		2.49	0.2***			
REC5	0.25		0.63		3.15	0.3***			

← Correlations →

1.Diverging	1				
2.Converging	0.46	1			
3.Power and Influence	0.65	0.27	1		
4.Openness	-0.42	-0.07	-0.13	1	

[a] The Mean Squares, Fs, and df are not shown in this table for the factors. For simplicity, I have included the ICCs for factors as part of this table.
[b] The Reliabilities shown here are those for each factor. The overall α = .92.
[c] IRRs were computed using the formula for multiple items (James, Damaree, & Wolf, 1984; 1993). The authors label this estimate as "r_{wg}."
***significant at p<.000, **significant at p<.005, *significant at p<.02
[d] These itesm were removed resulting in the final 30-items used in the final version of the TLI.

Using criteria established as standards of rigor for confirming a construct as one that is at the group or team level, we used intraclass correlations (ICCs) to determine if there would be convergence at the group level so as to verify team interaction as a group-level construct. ICCs were computed by running Analysis of Variance (ANOVA) studies using the formula for unequal groups (i.e., the harmonic mean[64] for the number of raters instead of the mean). The ICCs are also shown in table 1 for each dimension, all of which are significant at $p<.000$. The ICCs for the dimensions ranged from .2 to .5. These ICC values meet established standards of rigor to indicate that the dimensions are a group-level construct.

This is further verified using within-group agreement criteria (r_{wg}).[65] The results ranged from 0.76–0.96 (see last column in table 1), which indicates that the individual responses to each of the factors have strong within-group agreement as well. The thirty-five-item TLI has high reliability (Cronbach α =.92). The alphas for each dimension are also shown in table 1 and range from .75 to .94, which is well within the accepted range. These results show that team interaction as a construct is a group-level phenomenon.

B.3 Testing Our Measurement Model

We collected more data over the next two years and added the responses to the research sample used so as to obtain a sample size greater than 500. A total of 547 (83.9 percent of 652) participants took the TLI, of which 364 were males and 288 were females. One hundred and

[64] E. A. Haggard, *Intraclass Correlation and Analysis of Variance* (New York: Dryden Press, 1958), H. H. Harman, *Modern Factor Analysis*, 3rd ed. (Chicago: University of Chicago Press, 1976).

[65] L. R. James, R. G. Demaree, and G. Wolf, "Estimating Within-Group Interrater Reliability with and without Response Bias," *Journal of Applied Psychology* 69 (1984): 85–98; L. R. James, R. G. Demaree, and G. Wolf, "r_{wg}: An Assessment of Within-Group Interrater Agreement," *Journal of Applied Psychology* 78, no. 2 (1993): 306–9; D. A. Kenn and L. La Voie, "Separating Individual and Group Effects," *Journal of Personality and Social Psychology* 48, no. 2 (1985): 339–48; B. A. Schneider, A. N. Salvaggio, and M. Subirats, "Climate Strength: A New Direction for Climate Research," *Journal of Applied Psychology* 87, no. 2 (2002): 220–9; P. E. Shrout and J. L. Fleiss, "Intraclass Correlations: Uses in Assessing Rater Reliability," *Psychology Bulletin* 86 (1979): 420–8.

one teams were represented, with group sizes ranging from five to twenty-six. The sample had an average of 6.46 members (3.6 males and 2.89 females), with six groups made up entirely of men and ten groups entirely of women. Nonrespondent bias was not a problem, as the subjects who did not fill out the TLI had similar demographic data (including educational level) and level in the organization (primarily work groups). Four cases were removed due to excessive missing values, and two cases were removed that contained more than three outliers when running normality tests. The remaining 541 cases were acceptable for further analysis.

The four-factor model was tested using EFA, and it yielded the same four factors (scree-plots). However, after reviewing the items that had some cross-loadings against the original theoretical model and the initial study, we removed another five items that had loadings less than .4 or had cross-loadings greater than .25. The thirty items that remain are robust and much cleaner than the initial thirty-five items. The overall reliability of the scale is .89.

This final four-factor[66] (thirty-item) measurement model was used to run our CFA to establish goodness of fit with the final sample of 541 responses. Our final measurement model is a much better model, as demonstrated by the statistically significant change in X^2 ($DX^2_{(1)} = 68.298$) and better fit indexes. The initial structural model yielded an overall $X^2_{(11)}$ of 112.732, with NFI = .928, IFI = .934, CFI = .93, SRMR = .0683 and RMSEA = .137 (C.I. = .116-.160) whereas model 1 yielded an overall $X^2_{(10)}$ of 54.434, with NFI = .968, IFI = .974, CFI = .973, SRMR of .036; and RMSEA = .091 (C.I. = .068-.115). Table 2 below shows these results.

---

[66] J. Kim and C. W. Mueller, "Introduction to Factor Analysis: What It Is and How to Do It," *Sage University Paper Series in Quantitative Applications in the Social Sciences*, 07-013 (Thousand Oaks, CA: Sage Publications, 1978); J. C. Nunally, *Psychometric Theory*, 2nd ed. (New York: McGraw-Hill, 1978); E. J. Pedhazur and L. P. Schmelkin, *Measurement, Design, and Analysis: An Integrated Approach* (Hillsdale, NJ: Lawrence Erlbaum Associates, 1991); P. E. Spector, "Summated Rating Scale Construction," *Sage University Paper Series on Quantitative Applications in the Social Sciences*, 07-082 (Thousand Oaks, CA: Sage, 1992).

B.4 Testing Our Structural (Nomological) Validity with Widely Used Team Outcome Variables

The structural (nomological) validity of this construct (i.e. team interaction) is tested through demonstration of its impact on group effectiveness,[67] member satisfaction,[68] and psychological safety,[69] employing structural equation modeling. These three outcome variables were used, as they are common in team research. We ran the structural model using team interaction as a construct of the four factors (composites). The results of the initial model and model 1 (based on modification indices) are shown in table 2.

---

[67] R. J. Hackman, "The Design of Work Teams," in *Handbook of Organizational Behavior*, ed. J. Lorsch (Engelwood Cliffs, NJ: Prentice Hall, 1987), 315–42.

[68] J. G. Oetzel, "Self-Construals, Communication Processes, and Group Outcomes in Homogeneous and Heterogeneous Groups," *Small Group Research* 32, no. 1 (2001): 19–55.

[69] A. C. Edmondson, "Psychological Safety and Learning Behavior in Work Teams," *Administrative Science Quarterly* 44, no. 2 (1999): 350–83.

Table 2
Final Structural Model for Team Interaction (n=541)

FIT INDEX[a]	Initial Model	Model 1
χ^2(df)	122.732 (11)***	54.434(10)***
NFI	0.928	0.968
IFI	0.934	0.974
CFI	0.93	0.973
SRMR	0.0683	0.036
RSMEA	0.137	0.091
(90% CI)	.116-.160	.068-.115

Regression Weights (standard error) and Standardized Weights of Team Interaction on Dependent Variables				
Dependent Variables	Team Interaction		Team Interaction	
	B (s.e.)	β	B (s.e.)	β
Group Effectiveness	1.05 (.089)***	0.61***	1.09(.096)***	0.65***
Member Satisfaction	1.28 (.094)***	0.74***	1.33(.096)***	0.79***
Psychological Safety	1.23 (.093)***	0.72***	1.29(.095)***	0.76***

*** significant at p<.000

The parameter estimates show that team interaction has a strong and significant effect on group effectiveness (β= .65, p<.000), member satisfaction (β= .79, p<.000), and psychological safety (β= .76, p<.000). The final overall model (model 1) with the parameter estimates is shown in table 2. As can be seen in figure 1, team interaction affects all three outcome variables almost equally (with a slightly stronger effect on member satisfaction and psychological safety).

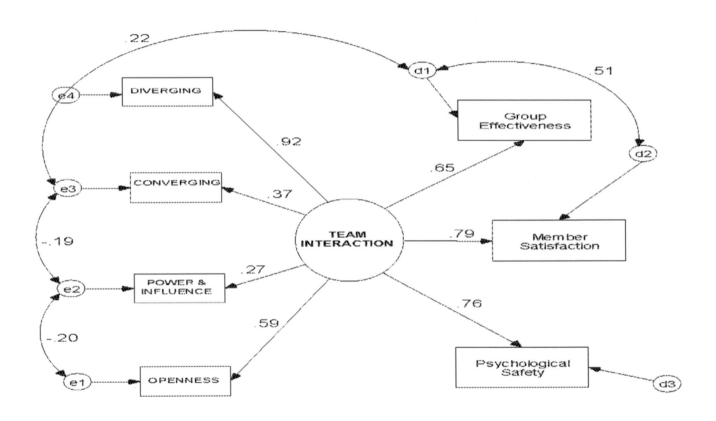

INDEX

functional (or departmental teams), 112–113

G

Gantt charts, 56
general systems theory, 159–160
goals, managing changing goals at the system level, 56–62
GoToMeeting, 4
Graduate Management Admissions Council, 100, 116, 153, 165
Guildford, J. P., 42

H

health care
nursing management course, 167–168
teams in, 115–116
high-impact engagement
achieving of at individual and interpersonal levels, 79–92
defined, 18, 173
formula for, 9, 23, 171
importance of, 11
high-impact teams (HITs), 16, 83, 84, 85, 86, 110

I

ideation process, 62, 63, 64, 65, 88
ideation tendency, 44
implementation/execution axis, 45, 68–73, 88
Individual Level, 23–103
individuality, as aspect of team interaction, 132–133, 149
information, as basic/major need, 26–27, 38, 44, 45, 46, 57, 58, 63, 70, 81
innovation
attending to at individual and team levels, 62

described, 43
effective innovation, 43
as having similar behavioral characteristics to creativity and design, 45
increasing emphasis on, 56
team's innovation, 151–152
innovation axis, 45, 62–68, 88
innovation tendencies, 76. *See also* execution tendencies
innovative capacity, 87, 88
Institute of Medicine, 115
interpersonal level, working effectively at, 79–81

J

Japan, concept of working with teams in, 161

K

Kolb, David, 13, 25, 37, 142

L

leadership, linking of to team leadership and team membership, 93
learning communities, as high-impact educational practice, 153
learning needs. *See also* basic/major needs; motivational learning needs
benefits of understanding and working with, 89
as motivational driver for human systems, 85–86
working with, 82–85
Learning Needs Inventory (LNI)
adaptability profile using, 41, 48
developing adaptability using, 73–75
development of, 26, 38, 185–191
focuses of, 94
in high-impact engagement formula, 9, 23, 171

importance of, 67

innovation and implementation tendencies in, 44

power of, 41

purpose of, 33, 37, 175

as tool for providing evidence-based training, 99–100

use of as launchpad for team training, coaching, and development, 97–98

use of for assessment of learning in educational institutions, 100–101

use of for training, coaching, and development, 96–97

use of in organizations and educational institutions, 52

utility of in organizations and educational institutions, 93–103

work motivation framework as applied to, 40

learning needs theory

of motivation, 45–51

shifting of at team level, 56–62

learning styles, 13–15, 25, 48. *See also specific learning styles*

Learning Styles Inventory (LSI), 13–15, 37, 38

linear model of change, 159

listening, knowing how to, 15–16

lower-level shifts (micro-level changes), 60

M

middle-level shifts (meso-level changes), 60

motivation theories, 38, 39–41, 45–51, 174

motivational learning needs. *See also* basic/major needs; learning needs

The Clarifier, 28–29, 46, 47

The Completer, 30–31, 46, 47

The Explorer, 26–27, 46, 47

LNI scores as showing four aspects of, 80

The Selector, 29–30, 46, 47

as underlying learning styles, 26

N

Newton, Isaac, 159

nonlinear dynamics, emergence of, 160

nursing management course, 167–168

O

open system, humans beings as, 85

openness, as dimension of team interaction, 130, 136, 149, 163, 177

organizational performance

ability to influence, 11, 94, 107

increase in, 120

organizational-level shifts (macro-level changes), 60

orientation, interpersonal exploration, and production, as model of team development, 159

other-awareness, 5–6

P

parameters, as basic/major need, 26, 29–31, 38, 44, 45, 46, 57, 65, 69, 81

Phase 1: Individual Level, 18, 23–103, 171, 174–175, 179, 180, 181

Phase 2: Team Level, 18, 105–170, 171, 176–179, 180, 182

phase models, 43, 44, 159

planning, as aspect of team interaction, 134–135, 149

power and influence, as dimension of team interaction, 89, 130, 135–136, 149, 153, 162, 177

principle of computational equivalence (PCE), 162

project management, 56, 89, 116, 119, 135, 145

project teams, 96, 100, 113, 114, 153

U

understanding, as aspect of team interaction, 133, 149
US News, 116

V

von Bertalanffy, Ludwig, 159

W

Wall Street Journal, 116
WebEx, 4
work improvement teams, 113, 159
work motivation, 16, 37, 38, 39–41, 51, 56, 57, 79, 174
World Report, 116

Z

Zoom, 4